C000042067

ClearRevise®

AQA GCSE
Spanish

Illustrated revision and practice

Foundation and Higher

Vivien Halksworth
Helena Gonzalez-Florido
John Halksworth

Published by
PG Online Limited
The Old Coach House
35 Main Road
Tolpuddle
Dorset
DT2 7EW
United Kingdom

sales@pgonline.co.uk
www.clearrevise.com
www.pgonline.co.uk
2024

PG ONLINE

PREFACE

Absolute clarity! That's the aim.

This is everything you need to ace your exams and beam with pride. Each topic is laid out in a beautifully illustrated format that is clear, approachable and as concise and simple as possible.

We have included worked examination-style questions with answers for each of the four papers. This helps you understand where marks are coming from and to familiarise yourself with the style of questions you will be asked. There is also a set of exam-style questions at the end of each section for you to practise your responses. You can check your answers against those given at the end of the book.

A full **transcript** and **audio clips** can be downloaded from the **clearrevise.com** website along with tips on how to approach the listening paper and guidance on marking each of the questions.

ACKNOWLEDGEMENTS

Every effort has been made to trace and acknowledge ownership of copyright. The publisher will be happy to make any future amendments with copyright owners that it has not been possible to contact. The publisher would like to thank the following companies and individuals who granted permission for the use of their images or material in this textbook.

Design and artwork: Jessica Webb / PG Online Ltd

All Sections
Photographic images: © Shutterstock
Football game © Abdul_Shakoor / Shutterstock, Running of the bulls © Migel / Shutterstock.com
Day of the Dead © Dina Julayeva / Shutterstock.com, La Tomatina © BearFotos / Shutterstock.com
Carnival © Alida_Garcia / Shutterstock.com, Beijing © Nahorski Pavel / Shutterstock.com

First edition 2024   10 9 8 7 6 5 4 3 2 1
A catalogue entry for this book is available from the British Library
ISBN: 978-1- 916518-02-5
Contributors: Vivien Halksworth, Helena Gonzalez-Florido and John Halksworth
Editor: Emma Brown
Copyright © PG Online 2024
All rights reserved

No part of this publication may be reproduced, stored in a retrieval system, or transmitted in any form or by any means without the prior written permission of the copyright owner.

This product is made of material from well-managed FSC®-certified forests and from recycled materials. Printed by Bell and Bain Ltd, Glasgow, UK.

THE SCIENCE OF REVISION

Illustrations and words

Research has shown that revising with words and pictures doubles the quality of responses by students.[1] This is known as 'dual-coding' because it provides two ways of fetching the information from our brain. The improvement in responses is particularly apparent in students when they are asked to apply their knowledge to different problems. Recall, application and judgement are all specifically and carefully assessed in public examination questions.

Retrieval of information

Retrieval practice encourages students to come up with answers to questions.[2] The closer the question is to one you might see in a real examination, the better. Also, the closer the environment in which a student revises is to the 'examination environment', the better. Students who had a test 2–7 days away did 30% better using retrieval practice than students who simply read, or repeatedly reread material. Students who were expected to teach the content to someone else after their revision period did better still.[3] What was found to be most interesting in other studies is that students using retrieval methods and testing for revision were also more resilient to the introduction of stress.[4]

Ebbinghaus' forgetting curve and spaced learning

Ebbinghaus' 140-year-old study examined the rate at which we forget things over time. The findings still hold true. However, the act of forgetting grammar and vocabulary and relearning them is what cements them into the brain.[5] Spacing out revision is more effective than cramming – we know that, but students should also know that the space between revisiting material should vary depending on how far away the examination is. A cyclical approach is required. An examination 12 months away necessitates revisiting covered material about once a month. A test in 30 days should have topics revisited every 3 days – intervals of roughly a tenth of the time available.[6]

Summary

Students: the more tests and past questions you do, in an environment as close to examination conditions as possible, the better you are likely to perform on the day. If you prefer to listen to music while you revise, listen to songs in Spanish. However, tunes without any lyrics will be far less detrimental to your memory and retention, and silence is most effective.[5] If you choose to study with friends, choose carefully – effort is contagious.[7]

1. Mayer, R. E., & Anderson, R. B. (1991). Animations need narrations: An experimental test of dual-coding hypothesis. *Journal of Education Psychology*, (83)4, 484–490.

2. Roediger III, H. L., & Karpicke, J.D. (2006). Test-enhanced learning: Taking memory tests improves long-term retention. *Psychological Science*, 17(3), 249–255.

3. Nestojko, J., Bui, D., Kornell, N. & Bjork, E. (2014). Expecting to teach enhances learning and organisation of knowledge in free recall of text passages. *Memory and Cognition*, 42(7), 1038–1048.

4. Smith, A. M., Floerke, V. A., & Thomas, A. K. (2016) Retrieval practice protects memory against acute stress. *Science*, 354(6315), 1046–1048.

5. Perham, N., & Currie, H. (2014). Does listening to preferred music improve comprehension performance? *Applied Cognitive Psychology*, 28(2), 279–284.

6. Cepeda, N. J., Vul, E., Rohrer, D., Wixted, J. T. & Pashler, H. (2008). Spacing effects in learning a temporal ridgeline of optimal retention. *Psychological Science*, 19(11), 1095–1102.

7. Busch, B. & Watson, E. (2019), *The Science of Learning*, 1st ed. Routledge.

CONTENTS

Theme 2 Popular culture

Theme 3 Communication and the world around us

Grammar

☑

Tiers, mark schemes and marking guidance

All of the Higher tier exam practice questions in this book have been marked with an **H** symbol. Foundation level questions have been marked with an **F**. Boundary level questions may have both **F H**.

The answers to exam questions should be marked in accordance with the mark schemes published on the AQA website. A set of guidance notes on how to interpret the mark schemes for each question type on each paper can be downloaded from **ClearRevise.com**. This also contains advice and tips on how to gain as many marks as you can.

Understanding the specification reference tabs

This number refers to the Theme number.
In this example, **Theme 2: Popular culture**.

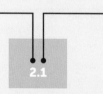

This number refers to the Topic number.
In this example, **Topic 1: Free-time activities**.

Downloading the speaking and listening clips

All of the MP3 audio clips can be downloaded from our website at ClearRevise.com/8692.

A full copy of the **transcripts** is also available to download.

TRACK 1

Scan the **QR code** here or on each question with a **listening or speaking symbol**.

Then select the **track** indicated.

THE BASICS

No vocabulary is specified for KS2 or KS3 so this section includes some key words and phrases that students at all levels will find helpful. This book makes no assumptions about vocabulary previously taught.

BASIC WORDS AND PHRASES

Los días de la semana — *The days of the week*

lunes	martes	miércoles	jueves	viernes	sábado	domingo
Monday	*Tuesday*	*Wednesday*	*Thursday*	*Friday*	*Saturday*	*Sunday*

! Notice that the days of the week do not have capital letters. Only **sábado** and **domingo** have different plural forms, e.g: **los sábados, los domingos.**

el fin de semana
the weekend

Useful phrases

el martes	on Tuesday		los jueves	on Thursdays
todos los viernes	every Friday		todos los días	every day
este fin de semana	this weekend		el viernes pasado	last Friday
la semana que viene	next week		el año próximo	next year
ayer	yesterday		hoy	today
mañana	tomorrow		la mañana	morning
anteayer	day before yesterday		pasado mañana	day after tomorrow
la tarde	afternoon / evening		la noche	night
mañana por la tarde	tomorrow afternoon		ayer por la mañana	yesterday morning
anoche	last night		esta noche	tonight
siempre	always		a veces	sometimes
nunca	never		a menudo	often

¿Qué hora es? — *What time is it?*

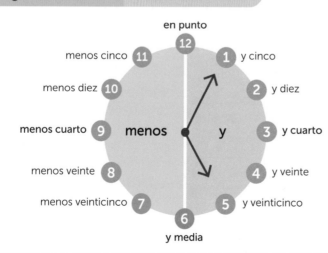

Es la una. *It's one o'clock.*

Son las dos. *It's two o'clock.*

Son las diez. *It's ten o'clock.*

Son las tres y cuarto.
It's quarter past three.

Son las cuatro menos veinte.
It's twenty to four.

A las nueve. *At nine o'clock.*

A las once y media de la noche.
At half past eleven at night.

Los meses y las estaciones del año — *The months and seasons of the year*

enero *January*	**febrero** *February*	**marzo** *March*
abril *April*	**mayo** *May*	**junio** *June*
julio *July*	**agosto** *August*	**septiembre** *September*
octubre *October*	**noviembre** *November*	**diciembre** *December*

! The months of the year do not have capital letters.

primavera *spring*

verano *summer*

otoño *autumn*

invierno *winter*

Mi cumpleaños es en marzo.	*My birthday is in March.*
En verano vamos a la costa.	*In summer we go to the coast.*
Hoy es el diecinueve de octubre.	*Today is the 19th October.*
Siempre vamos a Cádiz el dos de mayo.	*We always go to Cádiz on 2nd May.*

Los números — *Numbers*

1	uno/a	**11**	once	**21**	veintiuno/a	**31**	treinta y uno/a
2	dos	**12**	doce	**22**	veintidós	**42**	cuarenta y dos
3	tres	**13**	trece	**23**	veintitrés	**53**	cincuenta y tres
4	cuatro	**14**	catorce	**24**	veinticuatro	**64**	sesenta y cuatro
5	cinco	**15**	quince	**25**	veinticinco	**75**	setenta y cinco
6	seis	**16**	dieciséis	**26**	veintiséis	**86**	ochenta y seis
7	siete	**17**	diecisiete	**27**	veintisiete	**97**	noventa y siete
8	ocho	**18**	dieciocho	**28**	veintiocho	**100**	cien
9	nueve	**19**	diecinueve	**29**	veintinueve	**102**	ciento dos
10	diez	**20**	veinte	**30**	treinta	**112**	ciento doce

200	**300**	**400**	**500**	**600**
doscientos/-as	trescientos/-as	cuatrocientos/-as	quinientos/-as	seiscientos/-as
700	**800**	**900**	**1000**	**2000**
setecientos/-as	ochocientos/-as	novecientos/-as	mil	dos mil

! Numbers ending in **uno** and the ordinal numbers **primero** and **tercero** shorten before a masculine noun:

veintiuno → veintiún   primero → primer   tercero → tercer

+

first **primero/a**

second **segundo/a**

third **tercero/a**

in 2012 **en dos mil doce**

in 1987 **en mil novecientos ochenta y siete**

1 million **un millón**

Los colores *Colours*

marron	rojo/a	amarillo/a	verde	azul	blanco/a	gris	negro/a
brown	*red*	*yellow*	*green*	*blue*	*white*	*grey*	*black*

Expresiones importantes *Important expressions*

Hola. *Hello. / Hi.*

Buenos días. *Good morning.*

Buenas tardes. *Good afternoon / evening.*

Bienvenido/a/os/as. *Welcome.*

¿Qué tal? *How are you? / How's things?*

Adiós. *Goodbye.*

Buena suerte. *Good luck.*

Enhorabuena. *Congratulations.*

Por favor. *Please. / Excuse me.*

Gracias. *Thank you.*

Vale. *Okay.*   **De acuerdo.** *Alright. / Okay.*

Lo siento. *Sorry.*

(el) señor *Mr / (gentle)man / sir.*

(la) señora *Mrs / lady / madam.*

Opinions

Introduce your opinions with **Creo que... / Pienso que...** *I think that...* or **En mi opinión...** *In my opinion...* Then go on to develop your ideas using some of the following key phrases, or talk about your likes and dislikes.

Joining words

porque	así que	pero
because	*so*	*but*

para que
so that

Likes and dislikes

me gusta(n)	no me gusta(n)
I like	*I don't like*

me encanta(n)	odio
I love	*I hate*

! Note that you will need to use the subjunctive after **para que** – see **page 156**.

+ Remember

Remember that **gustar** and **encantar** don't work in quite the same way as the English 'like' and 'love'. See **pages 21** and **158–159**.

PHONICS

TRACK 1

These are the most important sounds in Spanish, where the pronunciation of letters is different from English. Listen to the recorded examples, and then have a go yourself. Each will be spoken twice followed by the examples

Letter	Sound	Examples
a	Open, like 'a' in 'hat' (never like the 'a' sounds in 'drama').	casa, alta
e	Open, like 'eh' sounds in English.	enfermo, verde
i	Like 'ee' in English.	increíble, italiano
o	Open, like the 'o' in 'pot'.	ojo, otoño
u	Like 'oo' in English.	uniforme, usar
ll	Like 'li' in 'million'. (Can sound like 'y' or 'j' in some parts of Spain or 'sh' in some parts of South America.)	llamar, calle
ch	A hard 'ch' sound like in 'chat'.	chico, leche
ca, co cu	When 'c' is followed by 'a', 'o' or 'u', it has a hard 'k' sound.	calor, común cultura
cu + vowel	This is pronounced like 'kw'.	cuando, acuerdo, cuidar
ce ci	When followed by 'e' or 'i', the 'c' is soft like 'th' in 'thin'. (Pronounced like 's' in Latin America and some parts of Spain.)	once, centro bicicleta
z	'Z' is pronounced like the 'c' in 'ce' or 'ci', as above (and like 's' in Latin America and some parts of Spain).	zapato, azul
que qui	The 'u' is not pronounced, so the sounds are 'keh' and 'kee'.	que, pequeño esquina, equipo
ga go gu	When 'g' is followed by 'a', 'o' or 'u', it has a hard sound, just like the English 'g' in 'good'.	gato hago gustar
ge gi	When 'g' is followed by 'e' or 'i', it has a soft sound coming from the back of the mouth. It is like the 'ch' in the Scottish word 'loch'.	general, coger colegio, gimnasio
gue gui	The 'u' is here to make the 'g' sound hard (like 'g' in 'good'). It is not pronounced.	hamburguesa seguir
j	The letter 'j' is like the 'ch' in the Scottish word 'loch'.	jamón, julio, mejor
ñ	This sound is like the 'ni' in 'onion'.	año, compañero
v	This sound can be as hard as a 'b', especially when it is the first letter in a word.	varios, verde, vamos, lavar
-r- -r	The 'r' sound is softer than the English sound, and the tongue touches the palate just behind the teeth.	pero, caro, moreno hablar
rr initial r n, l, s + r	This is a strong, rolled 'r' sound.	perro, aburrido rato, responsable sonrisa, alrededores
h	The letter 'h' is silent.	hospital, hambre

TOPICS FOR THEME 1
People and lifestyle

Specification coverage

Topic 1   Identity and relationships with others
Topic 2   Healthy living and lifestyle
Topic 3   Education and work

Information about the four papers for Foundation ⓕ and Higher ⓗ tiers:

Paper 1 – Listening

Written exam:
35 minutes ⓕ, 45 minutes ⓗ
40 marks ⓕ, 50 marks ⓗ
25% of GCSE

The recording is controlled by the invigilator with built-in repetitions and pauses.

Each exam includes 5 minutes' reading time at the start of the question paper before the listening material is played and 2 minutes at the end of the recording to check your work.

Section A – Listening comprehension questions in English, to be answered in English or non-verbally (ⓕ 32 marks, ⓗ 40 marks).

Section B – Dictation where students transcribe 4 sentences (ⓕ 8 marks) or 5 sentences (ⓗ 10 marks).

Paper 2 – Speaking

Non-exam assessment (NEA):
7–9 minutes ⓕ or 10–12 minutes ⓗ +
15 minutes' supervised preparation time
50 marks, 25% of GCSE

Role play – 10 marks, 1-1.5 minutes. ⓕ ⓗ

Reading aloud passage and short conversation – 15 marks.
Recommended time 2-2.5 minutes ⓕ and 3-3.5 minutes ⓗ.
Minimum 35 words ⓕ and minimum 50 words ⓗ.

Photo card discussion (two photos) – 25 marks.
Photo card discussion time:
4-5 minutes ⓕ and 6-7 minutes ⓗ.

Paper 3 – Reading

Written exam: 45 minutes ⓕ, 1 hour ⓗ
50 marks, 25% of GCSE

Section A – Reading comprehension questions in English, to be answered in English or non-verbally (40 marks).

Section B – Translation from Spanish into English, minimum of 35 words ⓕ or 50 words ⓗ (10 marks).

Paper 4 – Writing

Written exam: 1 hour 10 minutes ⓕ,
1 hour 15 minutes ⓗ
50 marks, 25% of GCSE

Set of three short writing tasks. ⓕ only. 25 marks.

Translation of sentences from English into Spanish, minimum 35 words ⓕ, or 50 words ⓗ (10 marks).

Produce a piece of writing in response to three compulsory bullet points, approximately 90 words in total. Choose from two questions (15 marks). ⓕ ⓗ

Open-ended writing task.
Two compulsory bullet points, approximately 150 words in total. Choose from two questions. (25 marks). ⓗ only.

MY FAMILY AND I

Hablando de ti y de tu familia   *Talking about yourself and your family*

Los miembros de la familia   *Members of the family*

el padre *father*	el padrastro *stepfather*	la madre *mother*	la madrastra *stepmother*	el abuelo *grandfather*	la abuela *grandmother*	el tío *uncle*

el hermano, el hermanastro *brother, stepbrother / half-brother*	la hermana, la hermanastra *sister, stepsister / half-sister*	el primo / la prima *cousin*	la tía *aunt*

+ Remember

Remember to make the masculine word plural to create 'parents', 'grandparents', etc:
los padres *parents* **OR** *fathers*, **los abuelos** *grandparents* **OR** *grandfathers*, **los hermanos** *brothers and sisters* **OR** *brothers*, **los tíos** *uncles and aunts* **OR** *uncles*.

Introductions

Me llamo ... *My name is ...*	Se llama ... *His / her name is ...*	Soy ... *I am ...*	Es ... *He / she is ...*	Tengo ... *I have ...*	Tiene ... *He / she has ...*

Mi cumpleaños es ... *My birthday is ...*	Su cumpleaños es ... *His / her birthday is ...*	Vivo en ... *I live in ...*	Vive en ... *He / she lives in ...*

Tengo ... años. *I am ... (years old).*	Tiene ... años. *He / she is ... (years old).*

1. Match the questions to the answers.

1.1	¿Cómo te llamas?		A	Tres, dos hermanos y una hermanastra.
1.2	¿Cuál es tu nacionalidad?		B	Tengo dieciséis años.
1.3	¿Cuántos años tienes?		C	Me llamo David.
1.4	¿Cuándo es tu cumpleaños?		D	En una ciudad en el norte de España.
1.5	¿Cuántos hermanos tienes?		E	Soy español.
1.6	¿Dónde vives?		F	Es el 13 de agosto.

1.1 C   1.2 E   1.3 B   1.4 F   1.5 A   1.6 D

2. Listen to these people (2.1–2.6) introducing a member of their family.

Complete the table in **English**.

TRACK 2

	Relationship to speaker and name	Age	Birthday	Where they live
2.1				
2.2				
2.3				
2.4				
2.5				
2.6				

*2.1 Father – José, 42, 20th January, Barcelona   2.2 Stepmother – Laura, 39, 14th July, Valencia
2.3 Brother – Pablo, 13, 2nd May, Málaga   2.4 Grandfather – Antonio, 78, 30th March, Madrid
2.5 Aunt – Sandra, 50, 11th October, Granada   2.6 Cousin – Carlos, 19, 27th February, Santander*

3. Check back to the questions on **page 8** and think about how you would answer them.

Now play the recording to hear the questions and pause after each one to give yourself time to answer.

TRACK 3

Vocabulary for nationality

inglés / inglesa	escocés / escocesa
English	*Scottish*

galés / galesa	irlandés / irlandesa
Welsh	*Irish*

PHYSICAL APPEARANCE

Describiendo el aspecto físico *Describing physical appearance*

Vocabulary

Hair

el pelo	*hair*
marrón	*brown*
negro	*black*
rubio	*blonde*
pelirrojo	*red*

Eyes

los ojos	*eyes*
azules	*blue*
verdes	*green*
marrones	*brown*
grises	*grey*

Build

alto/a	*tall*
bajo/a	*short*
gordo/a	*fat*
delgado/a	*thin*

---

1. Match the descriptions 1–4 with the correct picture.

 A   B   C   D

1.1 Tiene el pelo pelirrojo y los ojos verdes.
1.2 Tiene el pelo marrón y los ojos grises.
1.3 Tiene el pelo gris y los ojos azules.
1.4 Tiene el pelo rubio y los ojos marrones.

1.1C   1.2A   1.3B   1.4D

Adjectives

Adjectives are 'describing' words such as 'tall', 'large', 'green' or 'happy'. In Spanish they always agree with the noun they describe, so that means they can be masculine, feminine, singular and plural. They are usually positioned after the noun they describe.

This is how to make them agree:

Ending	M. singular	F. singular	M. plural	F. plural
-o	–o alto	–a alta	–os altos	–as altas
-e	–e verde	–e verde	–es verdes	–es verdes
consonant e.g. -l, -s, -n	–l azul	–l azul	–les azules	–les azules

!

Note that **marrón** loses its accent in the plural:
→ **marrones**.

Adjectives ending in **-z** change the **z** to a **c** in the plural:
feliz → felices.

2. Complete the sentences with the correct form of the adjectives.

 2.1 Mis hermanos son _____ (bajo) y _____ (delgado).

 2.2 Tengo dos gatos _____ (negro) y _____ (gordo).

 2.3 Mi prima es _____ (rubio) y tiene los ojos _____ (gris).

 2.4 Mis madres son _____ (alto) y las dos tienen el pelo _____ (marrón).

 2.5 Mi padrastro tiene los ojos _____ (verde) y el pelo _____ (negro).

 2.6 Mis caballos son _____ (marrón) y muy _____ (grande).

> **el gato** *cat*   **el perro** *dog*   **el caballo** *horse*

2.1 bajos / delgados   2.2 negros / gordos   2.3 rubia / grises   2.4 altas / marrón
2.5 verdes / negro   2.6 marrones / grandes

··· *Adjectives* **continued**

Adjectives of nationality that end in **-o** have the same **-o**, **-a**, **-os**, **-as** endings as other adjectives (e.g. **chino**, **china**, **chinos**, **chinas**). Note that they do not begin with a capital letter.

Others have different rules:

	M. singular	F. singular	M. plural	F. plural
English	inglés	inglesa	ingleses	inglesas
Spanish	español	española	españoles	españolas
French	francés	francesa	franceses	francesas
German	alemán	alemana	alemanes	alemanas

3. Take a little time to think about the vocabulary you need, then describe the people in the photos.

| Emma, age 3, Irish | Ana, age 19, Spanish | Hans, age 32, German | Jules, age 27, French |

> **las gafas** *glasses*   **rizado** *curly*   **liso** *straight*   **una barba** *a beard*

PERSONALITY

Describiendo la personalidad   *Describing personality*

Useful vocabulary

activo/a	*active*	gracioso/a	*funny*	positivo/a	*positive*
ambicioso/a	*ambitious*	hablador/ora	*chatty*	práctico/a	*practical*
animado/a	*lively*	listo/a	*clever*	responsable	*responsible*
capaz	*capable*	loco/a	*crazy*	serio/a	*serious*
comprensivo/a	*understanding*	nervioso/a	*nervous*	simpático/a	*nice / friendly*
deportivo/a	*sporty*	optimista	*optimistic*	trabajador/ora	*hard-working*
fiel	*loyal*	perezoso/a	*lazy*	tranquilo/a	*calm / laid-back*

Note that **-ista** adjectives (**optimista**, **realista**) only have two endings: **-ista** for masculine and feminine singular, **-istas** for masculine and feminine plural.

Adjectives ending in **-or** (**trabajador**, **hablador**) have the following endings: **trabajador** (masculine singular), **trabajadora** (feminine singular), **trabajadores** (masculine plural), **trabajadoras** (feminine plural).

1. Listen to Laura talking about members of her family.

   Which **three** adjectives are used to describe each member (1.1–1.6)?
   Answer in **English**.

   1.1 Capable, practical, responsible.   1.2 Serious, hard-working, ambitious.   1.3 Nice, positive, understanding.   1.4 Funny, clever, active.   1.5 Lively, sporty, chatty.   1.6 Nervous, crazy, loyal.

2. Read about Hugo and use his description to help you write a similar description of yourself.

   Hola, me llamo Hugo y soy español, de Sevilla. Tengo diecisiete años y mi cumpleaños es el 15 de abril. Soy bastante alto y tengo el pelo corto y negro y los ojos marrones.

   Creo que soy una persona simpática, en general, y tengo una actitud optimista. Yo pienso que tengo una personalidad tranquila, pero mis padres dicen que soy un poco perezoso.

   bastante *quite*   **la persona** *person*   **la actitud** *attitude*
   mis padres / amigos dicen que *my parents / friends say that*

Adjectives with ser and estar

When you use the verb **ser** with an adjective to describe someone or something (**es triste**, **eres muy serio**), it means that the characteristic is part of their personality.

When you use the verb **estar** with an adjective, it implies that they are being like that at that moment, because something has made them behave that way.

- **Es muy serio.** → *He is very serious.* (A serious person)
- **Está muy serio.** → *He is very serious.* (Implying something must be wrong or must have happened)
- **El gato es muy nervioso.** → *The cat is nervous.* (A timid, nervous sort of cat)
- **Hay fuegos artificiales; el gato está nervioso.** → *There are fireworks; the cat is nervous.*

---

3. ❺ Complete each sentence with either es or está.

   3.1 Miguel _____ muy animado hoy. ¿Por qué?

   3.2 Carlos practica muchos deportes; _____ muy deportivo.

   3.3 Gemma _____ bastante tranquila esta mañana; eso no es normal.

   3.4 ¡Qué guapa _____ Olivia! ¿Es una ocasión especial?

   3.5 Mi amigo Martín _____ guapo y elegante.

   3.6 Julio _____ un poco serio, ¿hay algún problema?

3.1 está   3.2 es   3.3 está   3.4 está   3.5 es   3.6 está

Dictation

4. You will hear **five** sentences, repeated **three** times.
   Write them down in **Spanish**.
   (**Note:** The Foundation ❺ paper will have only **four** sentences.)

   TRACK 5

   4.1 Tu cumpleaños / es el quince / de diciembre.

   4.2 Mi hermano / tiene los ojos / azules.

   4.3 Soy serio, / trabajador / y responsable.

   4.4 Tengo el pelo / largo y marrón.

   4.5 La abuela / está muy tranquila / hoy.

See the AQA website for the official mark schemes for all types of question or download the marking guidance from **ClearRevise.com**

✚ Remember

In Spanish, if you hear the sound 'th', as in the English word 'thin', remember this rule:

It will be spelt with a **z** if the following letter is **a**, **o** or **u** (**zapato**, **zona**, **azul**).

It will be spelt with a **c** if the following letter is **e** or **i** (**hacer**, **noticia**).

RELATIONSHIPS

¿Cómo te llevas con ...?   *How do you get on with ...?*

Izan

Me llevo muy bien con mi familia. Mi madre y mi padrastro me tratan bien y la vida en casa es muy cómoda. No tengo nada de qué quejarme.

Marco

Mi hermano menor es muy tonto y me molesta un montón. No nos llevamos nada bien y siempre nos peleamos por cualquier cosa.

Julia

Me relaciono muy bien con mi hermana. Tenemos muchas cosas en común y nos gustan las mismas cosas. ¡Tengo mucha suerte!

Lucía

Hay una nueva chica en mi clase y todas mis amigas se llevan bien con ella. Pero a mí no me gusta nada. No tengo confianza en ella, me parece falsa y no sé si es honesta.

Useful vocabulary

llevarse bien / mal con	*to get on well / badly with*		tener suerte	*to be lucky*
relacionarse con	*to relate to / get on with*		molestar	*to annoy*
tratar	*to treat*		pelearse	*to argue / fight*
cómodo	*comfortable*		cualquier cosa	*anything*
quejarse	*to complain*		confianza	*confidence / trust*

1. Who ...

   1.1 ...says they feel lucky?
   1.2 ...gets cross with a member of the family?
   1.3 ...is uncomfortable about a new acquaintance?
   1.4 ...feels they are well treated?
   1.5 ...shares interests with a member of the family?
   1.6 ...has arguments?
   1.7 ...says they can't complain?
   1.8 ...mentions a feeling of distrust?

1.1 Julia
1.2 Marco
1.3 Lucía
1.4 Izan
1.5 Julia
1.6 Marco
1.7 Izan
1.8 Lucía

Giving reasons

When you talk about how you get on with people, you will need to say why. The simplest way to do this is to add **porque** *because* and then your reason.

Me llevo bien con ... Me relaciono bien con ...		es generoso/a, simpático/a, comprensivo/a, gracioso/a, animado/a, alegre tiene una actitud positiva, optimista, tolerante
No me llevo bien con ... No me relaciono bien con ...	porque	es demasiado serio/a, aburrido/a, tonto/a, pesado/a, horrible tiene una actitud negativa
Mi ... y yo nos llevamos bien		tenemos mucho en común tenemos el mismo sentido del humor

2. Choose **two** people, one who you get on with and one who you do **not** get on with.

   Use the ideas on these two pages to write a few sentences about each one.
   Remember to give reasons and vary your language.

Possessive adjectives

You have been using **mi** and **mis** to say 'my'. Here is the full list of possessive adjectives. Note that they agree with the <u>following</u> noun.

	Followed by singular noun	Followed by plural noun
My	mi	mis
Your (one owner)	tu	tus
His / her / its / their, your (formal)	su	sus
Our	nuestro / nuestra	nuestros / nuestras
Your (more than one owner)	vuestro / vuestra	vuestros / vuestras

3. Complete the sentences with the correct possessive adjective.

   3.1 ¿Cómo te llevas con _____ hermanos?

   3.2 Nos llevamos bien con _____ profesores.

   3.3 Leo no tiene nada en común con _____ hermanas.

   3.4 Tenéis una buena relación con _____ abuelos.

   3.5 Ana piensa que _____ madre es guay.

   3.6 No me llevo bien con _____ primos.

   3.1 tus   3.2 nuestros   3.3 sus   3.4 vuestros
   3.5 su   3.6 mis

4. Read aloud the following passage and then listen to the recording of it.

TRACK 6

Me llevo muy bien con mi hermano porque tenemos mucho en común. Es gracioso y generoso y hacemos muchas cosas juntos. Mucha gente se pelea con su familia, pero yo no. Tengo suerte.

FRIENDS

¿Cómo es el amigo ideal? *What is the ideal friend like?*

Here are some useful phrases to describe what makes a good friend.

Un buen amigo ...	A good friend ...
te escucha cuando tienes un problema.	*listens to you when you have a problem.*
siempre guarda tus secretos.	*always keeps your secrets.*
es alguien de quien puedes depender.	*is someone you can depend on.*
es alguien en quien puedes confiar.	*is someone you can trust.*
siempre está allí si necesitas ayuda.	*is always there if you need help.*
te dice la verdad.	*tells you the truth.*
comparte tus intereses.	*shares your interests.*
te hace reír cuando estás triste.	*makes you laugh when you are sad.*

Forming the regular present tense

Take the infinitive of the verb you want. The infinitive is the main form of the verb and ends in **-ar**, **-er** or **-ir**.

Remove the **-ar**, **-er** or **-ir**:

escuchar *to listen* → **escuch-**

depender *to depend* → **depend-**

compartir *to share* → **compart-**

Then add the correct ending:

	Endings		
	-ar	-er	-ir
I	-o	-o	-o
You (singular)	-as	-es	-es
He / she / it / you (formal)	-a	-e	-e
We	-amos	-emos	-imos
You (plural)	-áis	-éis	-ís
They	-an	-en	-en

➕ Remember

Remember to learn the formation of the present tense – it is the tense you will need most of all.

1. A radio programme is doing a documentary about friendship and has interviewed these young people in the street.

    TRACK 7

    What does each one say about the ideal friend? Answer in **English**.

    1.1 Martín _____

    1.2 Lucía _____

    1.3 Bruno _____

    1.4 Emma _____

    1.5 Carlos _____

    1.1 *Someone who makes you laugh*

    1.2 *Is always there when you need them*

    1.3 *Always tells you the truth*

    1.4 *Always keeps your secrets*

    1.5 *Listens when you need to talk*

2. Amelia has written to a magazine to nominate her friend for a friendship award. Read what she has written and select the correct verb from the list to fill each gap.

ayuda	compartimos	dice	es	está
guarda	hace	llevamos	tiene	tenemos

Yo recomiendo a mi amiga, Alicia, para el premio porque (2.1) _____ la mejor amiga del mundo. Siempre (2.2) _____ allí cuando la necesito y siempre (2.3) _____ tiempo para escucharme si tengo un problema. Cuando tengo dificultades con mis deberes, Alicia me (2.4) _____ y si estoy triste, me (2.5) _____ reír. Sé que puedo confiar en ella porque siempre me (2.6) _____ los secretos. También dependo de ella porque me (2.7) _____ la verdad. Nos (2.8) _____ muy bien porque (2.9) _____ mucho en común y (2.10) _____ muchos intereses.

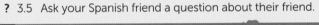
2.1 es   2.2 está   2.3 tiene   2.4 ayuda   2.5 hace   2.6 guarda   2.7 dice   2.8 llevamos
2.9 tenemos   2.10 compartimos

Role play

3. **F H** You are talking to a Spanish friend. Use what you have learned to prepare answers to these questions. Play the recording and pause after each question to give yourself time to answer. When you see this – **?** – you will have to ask a question.

TRACK 8

3.1 Say what you think the ideal friend is like. (Give **one** detail.)

3.2 Say what your best friend looks like. (Give **two** details.)

3.3 Describe your best friend's character. (Give **one** detail.)

3.4 Say why you and your friend get on. (Give **one** detail.)

? 3.5 Ask your Spanish friend a question about their friend.

Don't use up valuable preparation time thinking up more details than you need.

Give only the amount of detail stated.

Download the marking guidance at **ClearRevise.com**.

IDENTITY AND RELATIONSHIPS WITH OTHERS

Ponerlo todo junto   *Putting it all together*

1. Olivia has written about her friends and family.
   Read what she says and answer the questions below.

> No es posible decir si me importan más mis amigos o mi familia; los dos son igualmente esenciales en mi vida, por razones diferentes.
>
> Tengo una familia muy cariñosa y feliz, y sé que tengo mucha suerte. Me encanta pasar tiempo con ellos y siempre lo pasamos bien cuando vamos de excursión o de vacaciones. Me gusta ir al centro comercial con mi madre; siempre decide comprarme algo o me lleva a una cafetería para comer. Mi padre y yo tenemos muchas cosas en común y tenemos muchas conversaciones interesantes sobre películas y novelas.
>
> Pero, claro, hay algunas cosas que siempre prefieres hacer con los amigos. Mis padres no tienen ni idea sobre música moderna, por ejemplo, o las últimas tendencias de la moda. Y claro, hay ciertas cosas que les digo a mis amigos que nunca diría a mis padres.

1.1 Who is most important to Olivia?   **A** Friends   **B** Family   **C** Both friends and family

1.2 Why does she think she is lucky?   **A** Great friends   **B** Loving family   **C** Lots of reasons

1.3 What does she like doing with her mother?   **A** Shopping   **B** Cooking   **C** Chatting

1.4 What does she share with her father?   **A** Trips out   **B** Sense of humour   **C** Same interests

1.5 What is one thing she would not discuss with her parents?   **A** Homework   **B** Fashion   **C** Friends

1.1 C   1.2 B   1.3 A   1.4 C   1.5 B

Reading aloud

2. Read this passage aloud and then listen to the recording of it.

TRACK 9

> Mi hermano mayor es un chico muy gracioso y tiene un buen sentido del humor. Tiene el pelo marrón y los ojos azules. Se llama Mateo y en su tiempo libre juega al baloncesto.

! Think carefully about how to pronounce **a**, **j**, **ch**, **ci**, **h**, **z**, **ll**, **e** and **ce**. See **page 5**.

3. Look at the response to the exam question below.

You are writing an article about yourself and your family.

Write approximately **90 words** in **Spanish**.

You must write something about each bullet point.

Mention:
- your appearance
- your personality
- how you get on with the different members of your family.

In the exam, these questions will require three time frames.

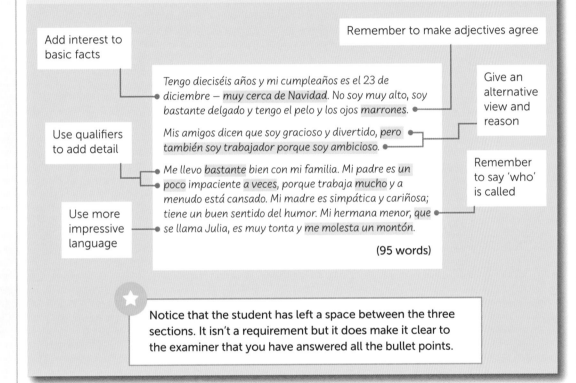

Add interest to basic facts

Remember to make adjectives agree

Tengo dieciséis años y mi cumpleaños es el 23 de diciembre – muy cerca de Navidad. No soy muy alto, soy bastante delgado y tengo el pelo y los ojos marrones.

Give an alternative view and reason

Use qualifiers to add detail

Mis amigos dicen que soy gracioso y divertido, pero también soy trabajador porque soy ambicioso.

Me llevo bastante bien con mi familia. Mi padre es un poco impaciente a veces, porque trabaja mucho y a menudo está cansado. Mi madre es simpática y cariñosa; tiene un buen sentido del humor. Mi hermana menor, que se llama Julia, es muy tonta y me molesta un montón.

Remember to say 'who' is called

Use more impressive language

(95 words)

Notice that the student has left a space between the three sections. It isn't a requirement but it does make it clear to the examiner that you have answered all the bullet points.

¡Ahora te toca a ti!   *Now it's your turn!*

4. You are writing an article about friends.

Write approximately **90 words** in **Spanish**.

You must write something about each bullet point.

Mention:
- the best qualities of your friends
- what you like to do together
- reasons that you sometimes have arguments.

FOOD AND DRINK

Las comidas y las horas de comer   *Meals and mealtimes*

1. Read Elena's description of her family meals. Answer the questions in **English**.

> Tomo el desayuno a las siete y media y normalmente tomo tostadas con un vaso de leche. Mis padres toman café, y mi hermano un chocolate caliente. En el instituto tomo un bocadillo de jamón o queso durante el recreo. Comemos en casa a las dos y media. A menudo hay pollo con verduras, o pescado con patatas fritas. Mis comidas favoritas son la paella (me encantan los platos de arroz) y las hamburguesas con ensalada, pero sin tomates porque no me gustan. Cenamos a las nueve; para la cena tomamos algo ligero como una tortilla. Comemos bastante fruta en nuestra casa, sobre todo manzanas, naranjas y uvas.

1.1 What time is breakfast?

1.2 What does Elena have for breakfast?

1.3 What does she have at break at school?

1.4 What time is lunch at home?

1.5 What two meals do they often have for lunch?

1.6 Why does Elena like paella?

1.7 What is her other favourite dish?

1.8 What does she not like?

1.9 What time is the evening meal?

1.10 How does she describe the meal?

1.11 What is a typical evening meal?

1.12 What fruit do they eat a lot of?

1.1 7.30 am   1.2 Toast and a glass of milk   1.3 A ham or cheese sandwich   1.4 2.30 pm
1.5 Chicken and vegetables, fish and chips   1.6 She loves rice dishes.   1.7 Burgers and salad
1.8 Tomatoes   1.9 9.00 pm   1.10 Light   1.11 Omelette   1.12 Apples, oranges and grapes

2. **H** Listen to these students who are talking in their Spanish class about their stay with families on a Spanish exchange.
Complete the sentences with the correct word.

TRACK 10

2.1 I love the (a) _____ , and the (b) _____ are better than in England.

2.2 The bread is different; it seems (c) _____ because they put (d) _____ in it.

2.3 They eat fewer (e) _____ and more (f) _____ .

2.4 The parents have a little (g) _____ with dinner and the children have (h) _____ .

(a) salads   (b) tomatoes   (c) sweet(er)   (d) sugar   (e) sweets   (f) fruit   (g) (glass of) wine   (h) water

Using gustar

The verb **gustar** seems tricky to use until you get used to it. The reason it seems complicated is that it actually means 'to please' and not 'to like'.

So when you want to say that you like chicken, you have to say that chicken pleases you!

And the word order is the opposite to English.

| Me | gusta | el pollo | $\longrightarrow$ | *Me* | *it pleases* | *chicken* |

So, use **me gusta** when what follows is a singular thing (**Me gusta el pescado** *I like fish*) or a verb (**Me gusta cocinar** *I like cooking*).

Use **me gustan** if what follows is plural: **Me gustan los huevos**. *I like eggs.* (This is because you are literally saying *They please me, eggs*).

> **!** Notice that you always use the article (**el, la, los, las**) with the noun when you are saying what you like.
>
> To say you don't like something, put **no** in front of **me gusta(n)**.

3. Translate these sentences into **Spanish**.

3.1 I like toast.

3.2 I don't like milk.

3.3 I like oranges.

3.4 I don't like ham.

3.5 I like eggs.

3.6 I don't like rice dishes.

3.7 I like cheese.

3.8 I don't like vegetables.

3.9 I like omelettes.

3.10 I don't like cooking.

3.1 *Me gustan las tostadas.*

3.2 *No me gusta la leche.*

3.3 *Me gustan las naranjas.*

3.4 *No me gusta el jamón.*

3.5 *Me gustan los huevos.*

3.6 *No me gustan los platos de arroz.*

3.7 *Me gusta el queso.*

3.8 *No me gustan las verduras.*

3.9 *Me gustan las tortillas.*

3.10 *No me gusta cocinar.*

EATING HEALTHILY

¿Qué es una dieta sana? — *What is a healthy diet?*

Useful vocabulary

el aceite	oil	la fruta	fruit
el agua (f)	water	la grasa	fat / grease
el alcohol	alcohol	mediterráneo/a	Mediterranean
el azúcar	sugar	el pescado	fish
los caramelos	sweets	el postre	dessert
la carne	meat	el régimen	(special) diet
el cuerpo	body	la sal	salt
cuidar	to look after	saludable	healthy
la dieta	diet	sano/a	healthy
dulce	sweet	vegano/a	vegan
la ensalada	salad	vegetariano/a	vegetarian
equilibrado/a	balanced	las verduras	(green) vegetables

The word **agua** begins with a stressed **a**, so it sounds odd to say '**la agua**'. Instead, we say **el agua**, even though it is a feminine word. The same applies to **el hambre** *hunger* and **el aula** *classroom*.

¿Comes una dieta sana? — *Do you eat a healthy diet?*

Intento comer menos carne roja y más pescado y verduras. Lo más importante es tener una dieta equilibrada.

Intento reducir la sal y el azúcar en los productos que compro. También tomo más platos veganos.

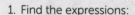

Quiero reducir la grasa en mi dieta. Por ejemplo, ya no pongo aceite en las ensaladas. También evito los caramelos.

Soy muy deportista y necesito cuidar mi cuerpo. Por eso, soy vegetariano y nunca tomo alcohol.

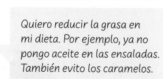

1. Find the expressions:

   1.1 I try to reduce
   1.2 the most important thing is
   1.3 I never have
   1.4 I also avoid
   1.5 to look after my body
   1.6 I try to eat less
   1.7 I no longer put
   1.8 a balanced diet
   1.9 vegan dishes
   1.10 the products I buy

   1.1 *intento reducir*   1.2 *lo más importante es*   1.3 *nunca tomo*   1.4 *también evito*
   1.5 *cuidar mi cuerpo*   1.6 *intento comer menos*   1.7 *ya no pongo*   1.8 *una dieta equilibrada*
   1.9 *platos veganos*   1.10 *los productos que compro*

Regular verbs in the first person singular of the present tense

Notice how regular verbs in the first person singular of the present tense tend to end in **-o**. This is true for regular verbs of all three categories, whether they are **-ar**, **-er** or **-ir** verbs.

tomar → tomo *I have*	evitar → evito *I avoid*	comer → como *I eat*	compartir → comparto *I share*
intentar → intento *I try*	comprar → compro *I buy*	beber → bebo *I drink*	decidir → decido *I decide*

There are a number of irregulars like **pongo** *I put*, **soy / estoy** *I am* and **tengo** *I have*. You will meet more irregulars in 1.2, Exercise and health, on **page 24**.

2. ⊕ Listen to these people (1–4) talking about their diets. Complete the table.

TRACK 11

	What is good about their diet?	What is bad about their diet?
Amira		
Manuel		
Isabel		
Adrián		

> **demasiado** *too much*   **bastante** *quite a lot*   **menos** *less*   **más** *more*   **un poco** *a little*
> **mejor** *better*   **peor** *worse*   **por otra parte / en cambio** *on the other hand*

Amira: good – drinks lots of water; bad – eats too many sweet things
Manuel: good – eats very little fat; bad – puts too much salt in/on food
Isabel: good – has a healthy breakfast every day; bad – eats too much red meat
Adrián: good – eats lots of fruit; bad – has too much fried food

Role play

3. 🇫 ⊕ You are talking to a Spanish friend. Use what you have learned to prepare answers to these questions. Play the recording and pause after each question to give yourself time to answer. Then listen to the example response. When you see this – **?** – you will have to ask a question.

TRACK 12

3.1 Say what you have for breakfast. (Give **two** details.)

3.2 Say what your favourite meal is. (Give **two** details.)

3.3 Say if you have a healthy diet. (Give **two** details.)

3.4 Say what you need to change about your diet. (Give **one** detail.)

? 3.5 Ask your Spanish friend a question about their diet.

EXERCISE AND HEALTH

What exercise do you do?

Useful vocabulary

Hago ...	
I do / go...	
natación	*swimming*
equitación	*horse riding*
ciclismo	*cycling*
atletismo	*athletics*
yoga	*yoga*

Juego ...	
I play...	
al fútbol	*football*
al baloncesto	*basketball*
al rugby	*rugby*
al bádminton	*badminton*
al tenis	*tennis*

Voy al gimnasio.	*I go to the gym.*
Doy un paseo.	*I go for a walk.*
Me voy a correr.	*I go running.*

1. Read what these young people do to keep fit and answer the questions below.

En el instituto hago atletismo en verano y juego al baloncesto en invierno. Con mis amigos prefiero jugar al tenis, y los domingos por la mañana doy un paseo con mi perro.
Leo

Juego al bádminton en el polideportivo los jueves y hago natación los sábados. Nunca voy al gimnasio porque lo encuentro aburrido. Cuando puedo, hago equitación en el campo.
Mariana

En el colegio juego al fútbol en el equipo femenino y los fines de semana hago ciclismo. Quiero probar el yoga porque parece relajante. A veces me voy a correr por la mañana.
Sofía

1.1 When does Leo play basketball in school?

1.2 When does he walk the dog?

1.3 When and where does Mariana play badminton?

1.4 Why doesn't she like going to the gym?

1.5 Where does she like going horse riding?

1.6 What is Sofía a member of at school?

1.7 When does she go cycling?

1.8 What does she want to try?

1.9 What does she sometimes do in the mornings?

1.10 Find the verbs *I play, I can, I prefer, I want*

1.1 in winter   1.2 Sunday mornings   1.3 at the sports centre on Thursdays
1.4 she finds it boring   1.5 in the country(side)   1.6 the girls' football team
1.7 at weekends   1.8 yoga   1.9 go running   1.10 juego, puedo, prefiero, quiero

Radical-changing verbs

These are verbs that have a spelling change in the present tense that affects four of the six parts of the verb. It is only the stem of the verb that is affected; the endings are the same as for regular verbs. This is how they behave:

encontrar (o → ue) to find	querer (e → ie) to want / love	pedir (e → i) to ask for
encuentro	quiero	pido
encuentras	quieres	pides
encuentra	quiere	pide
encontramos	queremos	pedimos
encontráis	queréis	pedís
encuentran	quieren	piden

! Note that with the verb **jugar** it is the **u**, not an **o**, that changes to **ue**.
For more about radical-changing verbs, see **page 149** in the grammar section.

2. Using the vocabulary from **page 24** and the information on radical-changing verbs, translate these sentences into **Spanish**.

2.1 I play football at the weekends.

2.2 I prefer to play badminton in school.

2.3 I want to try horse riding in the future.

2.4 I find yoga very relaxing.

2.5 I think that cycling is boring.

2.6 I can go to the gym in the sports centre.

2.7 She prefers to go for a walk.

2.8 We want to try athletics.

2.1 Juego al fútbol los fines de semana. 2.2 Prefiero jugar al bádminton en el instituto / colegio. 2.3 Quiero probar la equitación en el futuro. 2.4 Encuentro el yoga muy relajante. 2.5 Creo que el ciclismo es aburrido. 2.6 Puedo ir al gimnasio en el centro de deportes / polideportivo. 2.7 Prefiere dar un paseo. 2.8 Queremos probar el atletismo.

3. Complete the sentences to talk about your activities. (They don't all have to be true!)

- En el instituto ...
- En verano ... pero en invierno ...
- Nunca ...
- A veces ...
- Quiero probar ...
- Con mis amigos prefiero ...

+ Remember

Remember that, after **prefiero**, you need the infinitive (e.g. **jugar** *to play*, **dar** *to give*, and **hacer** *to do*).

A HEALTHY LIFE

¿Llevas una vida sana?   *Do you lead a healthy lifestyle?*

1. Listen to these people (1.1–1.5), who are talking about the things they do that help them lead a healthy lifestyle.
Match each one to the correct option in the grid.

Options

Person 1.1: _____

Person 1.2: _____

Person 1.3: _____

Person 1.4: _____

Person 1.5: _____

A Finding ways to relax

B Getting enough sleep

C Growing their own food

D No technology before bed

E Protection from the sun

F Spending time outdoors

G Work-life balance

acostarse *to go to bed*
apagar *to turn off*
el correo electrónico *email*
descansar *to rest*
relajarse *to relax*
la crema solar *sun cream*

1.1 B   1.2 D   1.3 G   1.4 A   1.5 E

2. Read this article giving advice on what not to do if you want to lead a healthy lifestyle.

No recomendamos pasar todo el día en el sofá; si haces esto te sientes más cansado y te falta energía. Nunca debes trabajar o estudiar después de las nueve – no puedes dormir después porque tu cerebro es demasiado activo. Tampoco debes usar la tecnología en el dormitorio, ni siquiera la televisión – crea demasiada estimulación. Durante las horas de más calor, nadie debería estar al sol más de veinte minutos, sin ninguna excepción.

Find the negative phrases in the text:

(a) neither must you use   (b) you cannot sleep   (c) you must never work

(d) no one should be   (e) without any   (f) not even the TV   (g) we do not recommend

3. Answer the questions in **English**.

3.1 Why should you not spend all day on the sofa?

3.2 Why can't you sleep if you work late?

3.3 Why should you not use technology in the bedroom?

3.4 What is the 'rule' about being out in the hottest part of the day?

2. (a) tampoco debes usar   (b) no puedes dormir   (c) nunca debes trabajar
    (d) nadie debería estar   (e) sin ninguna   (f) ni siquiera la televisión   (g) no recomendamos

3. 3.1 You feel more tired and you lack energy.   3.2 Your brain is too active.
    3.3 It creates too much stimulation. 3.4 No one should be in the sun for more than 20 mins.

Negative expressions

You saw a lot of these expressions on **page 26**. This is how to use them.

Spanish	English	Example
no	*no* *not*	**No, no veo la tele en el dormitorio.** *No, I don't watch TV in the bedroom.*
nadie	*no one* *nobody*	**Nadie hace eso.** *No one does that.* **No hay nadie en la casa.** *There is no one in the house.*
nada	*nothing* *not ... anything*	**No tengo nada que hacer.** *I have nothing to do. / I haven't got anything to do.*
nunca	*never*	**Nunca trabajo después de las nueve.** *I never work after nine.*
ninguno / a	*none* *not ... any*	**No tengo ningún dinero.** *I haven't got any money. / I have no money.*
ya no	*no longer* *not ... anymore*	**Ya no como carne.** *I no longer eat meat. / I don't eat meat anymore.*
ni siquiera	*not even*	**¿Ni siquiera el pollo?** *Not even chicken?*
tampoco	*neither* *not ... either*	**Yo no como carne tampoco.** *I don't eat meat either.*
sin	*without*	**Prefiero el café sin leche.** *I prefer coffee without milk.*

> **!** **Ninguno** shortens to **ningún** before a masculine singular noun. It agrees as normal with a feminine singular noun: **No me gusta ninguna fruta.** *I don't like any fruit.*
>
> Notice how in negative sentences everything that can become negative does so! It is like using double negatives. **No hago nada los domingos** – literally *'I don't do nothing on Sundays'*.

4. Translate these sentences into **English**.

4.1 Nunca fumo porque es malo para la salud.

4.2 Nadie en mi familia come patatas fritas.

4.3 Ya no tomo mucha carne roja.

4.4 Nunca tomo postres, ni siquiera en restaurantes.

4.5 No pongo azúcar en el café tampoco.

4.6 No me gusta ninguna fruta.

4.7 Puedes hacer muchas comidas sin grasa.

4.1 I never smoke because it's bad for your health. 4.2 Nobody in my family eats chips / fries. 4.3 I don't have much red meat anymore. 4.4 I never have desserts, not even in restaurants. 4.5 I don't put sugar in coffee either. 4.6 I don't like any fruit. 4.7 You can make a lot of meals without fat.

GOOD INTENTIONS

Los buenos propósitos para el futuro — *Good intentions for the future*

1. The Gómez family post their resolutions on the kitchen noticeboard.
   Read them and answer the questions.

> Voy a tomar más pescado y menos carne roja.
>
> Mamá

> Voy a apagar mi móvil a las diez y media cada noche.
>
> Gabriela

> No voy a contestar mis correos electrónicos del trabajo los fines de semana.
>
> Papá

> Voy a decir 'no' a los postres y voy a comer menos pan.
>
> Rodrigo

> Papá, ¡tú vas a dejar de fumar, y yo voy a ayudarte!
>
> Alicia

Whose resolution ...

1.1   involves reducing calorie intake?
1.2   is not about themself?
1.3   is about work-life balance?
1.4   is an effort to improve sleep patterns?
1.5   involves making healthy protein choices?

1.1 Rodrigo   1.2 Alicia   1.3 Papá   1.4 Gabriela   1.5 Mamá

The immediate future tense

This future tense is probably the easiest tense in Spanish.

You take the correct part of the present tense of **ir** *to go*:

voy *I am going*

vas *you* (singular) *are going*

va *he / she / it is going, you* (formal) *are going*

vamos *we are going*

vais *you* (plural) *are going*

van *they / you* (formal) *are going*

then add **a** + the infinitive (**dar**, **ver**, **ir**)

2. Look back at the bottom of **page 28** to remind yourself of the formation of the immediate future tense. Now look at these sentences. There is **one** error in each sentence. Find it and say what the correct version should be.

2.1 Voy comer más verduras en el futuro. ✗

2.2 Mi padre vas a preparar más comidas vegetarianas. ✗

2.3 Mis hermanos y yo vamos a bebemos más agua. ✗

2.4 Mi familia van a dar más paseos en el campo. ✗

2.5 Yo ir a tomar fruta o yogur de postre. ✗

*2.1 The **a** is missing from **voy a comer**.   2.2 **Mi padre** (he) should be followed by **va**, not **vas**.*

*2.3 It should be **vamos a beber** (the second verb should be infinitive).*

*2.4 **Familia** is an 'it', so the verb is **va** not **van**.   2.5 **Ir** needs to be in the present tense → **voy**.*

3. Listen to these people (3.1–3.5) talking about their plans to improve their lifestyle. Which statements are correct? Choose statement **A** or **B**, or both statements **A** and **B**.   TRACK 14

3.1 **A.** He wants to eat earlier.   **B.** He wants to go to bed earlier.

3.2 **A.** She can't swim.   **B.** She is going to have swimming lessons.

3.3 **A.** They eat too much junk food.   **B.** He is going to shop at the market.

3.4 **A.** She is going to start jogging.   **B.** She spends too much time indoors.

3.5 **A.** He couldn't manage a vegan diet.   **B.** He is going to cut out meat.

3.1 A   3.2 A + B   3.3 A   3.4 B   3.5 A + B

4. Create as many sentences as you can using combinations of phrases from this word box.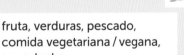

En el futuro, Empezando mañana,	voy a mi familia y yo vamos a	comer tomar beber	más	fruta, verduras, pescado, comida vegetariana / vegana, agua, leche
			menos	carne roja, postres, caramelos, grasa, comida frita, café, azúcar, hamburguesas
		hacer		más ejercicio comidas más sanas

HEALTHY LIVING AND LIFESTYLE

Ponerlo todo junto   *Putting it all together*

1. Read this article and decide which **five** statements are true.

> Los expertos recomiendan el estilo de vida mediterráneo por muchas razones. La primera es la dieta de la región, que consiste en abundantes frutas, verduras y legumbres, pan, aceite de oliva, poca carne y mucho pescado. Típicamente los postres consistían en fruta o yogur, y los caramelos son algo relativamente nuevo para los españoles.
>
> Sin embargo, no es solo por la comida que todos quieren vivir en el mediterráneo, es el estilo de vida también. Los españoles entienden la importancia de descansar después de comer, de evitar el sol durante las horas más calientes del día y de sacar una silla a la calle por la tarde para sentarse y hablar con los vecinos. No olvidemos la vida social de los pueblos con sus días festivos y sus fiestas que reúnen a todos y crean un fuerte sentido de comunidad.

A. The Mediterranean way of life is considered healthy just because of the diet.
B. Traditionally desserts were a healthy option.
C. Sweets did not used to be commonplace in Spain.
D. Spanish people love to eat outside in the sun.
E. They often go for a stroll after lunch.
F. People often sit out in the street to chat.
G. Town events bring people together.
H. There is a strong sense of community spirit.

True: B, C, F, G, H

2. ❶ Listen to these people (2.1–2.4) talking. What do they do that is a healthy habit and what do they do that is unhealthy? Select the correct letters from the grid.
TRACK 15

	Healthy	Unhealthy
2.1 Lorenzo		
2.2 Claudia		
2.3 Adrián		
2.4 Valeria		

A	vegetarian diet	F	sun protection
B	drinking water	G	not smoking
C	exercise	H	too much time indoors
D	shopping habits	I	work-life balance
E	sleep patterns	J	use of technology

2.1 Lorenzo: Healthy – D; unhealthy – E   *2.3 Adrián: Healthy – G; unhealthy – I*
2.2 Claudia: Healthy – B; unhealthy – J (I)   *2.4 Valeria: Healthy – C; unhealthy – H*

Photo card

3. Look at the two photos and make notes about what you can say about them. Then set a timer and talk about the content of the photos. You must say at least one thing about each photo.

   Foundation **F** students have **one minute** to talk and Higher **H** students have a **minute and a half**. Listen to the recording to hear a student talking about the photos.

Photo 1

Photo 2

Grammar gap fill

4. **F** Complete the following sentences in Spanish. Write the correct word in the space.

   4.1 No fumo, pero bebo _____ vino.   [ninguno / demasiado / algo]

   4.2 Me _____ mucho las ensaladas.   [gusto / gusta / gustan]

   4.3 Mi amigo Dani _____ al tenis.   [juega / jugar / juegas]

   4.4 Es un hábito horrible, _____ voy a fumar.   [nadie / nada / nunca]

   4.5 Voy a _____ más pescado en el futuro.   [como / tomar / preparando]

5. You are writing an article about how to lead a healthy lifestyle. Write approximately **90 words** in **Spanish**. You must write something about each bullet point. Mention:

   - how you keep fit
   - activities you will do in summer
   - the healthy food you ate last week

4.   *4.1 demasiado   4.2 gustan   4.3 juega   4.4 nunca   4.5 tomar*

5.   *Example answer:*

   Me siento mejor cuando hago ejercicio así que intento hacer deportes y actividades activas casi todos los días. Juego al fútbol en el colegio y voy a la piscina los domingos.

   En verano, mi hermano y yo jugaremos al tenis y vamos a dar paseos en el campo.

   También es importante comer bien. La semana pasada, preparé ensaladas para llevar al instituto para comer y comí fruta de postre. Mi familia y yo tomamos pollo y pescado con verduras para la cena y una tarde probamos un plato de pasta con salsa de tomate. ¡Muy rico!

   (96 words)

SCHOOL AND SCHOOL SUBJECTS

¿Qué asignaturas te gustan?   *What subjects do you like?*

Vocabulary

el inglés	English	el español	Spanish
el francés	French	el alemán	German
las matemáticas	Maths	las ciencias	Science
la biología	Biology	la química	Chemistry
la física	Physics	la geografía	Geography
la historia	History	el dibujo	Art
la religión	Religious studies / RE	la educación física	PE
la cocina	Cookery / Food Tech	el arte dramático	Drama
la informática	ICT	la música	Music

> **!** When you hear or see the word **física**, take a moment to check whether it has the word **educación** with it. It is easy to confuse 'Physics' with 'Physical Education' in Spanish.

1. Read these comments. Which subject does each student like best and least, and why?

Yo no tengo ningún talento creativo y por eso detesto las clases de dibujo. Mi asignatura favorita es la informática porque me gustan los ordenadores y creo que será muy útil en el mundo del trabajo. **María**

Odio el arte dramático porque no tengo mucha confianza y las clases me ponen incómodo. Me gusta bastante la educación física, pero prefiero la cocina. Quiero trabajar en un restaurante algún día. **Manuel**

No me gustan nada los idiomas. Me parecen muy difíciles y no puedo pronunciar el francés. Las asignaturas que me gustan más son las ciencias porque son muy lógicas e interesantes. **Paula**

Aunque me interesa la geografía, me encantan las lenguas extranjeras. Quiero estudiar inglés y alemán en la universidad porque espero tener una carrera en turismo. No me gusta nada la música porque canto muy mal. **David**

*María – likes ICT (likes computers and thinks it will be useful for work). Dislikes art (has no creative talent). **Manuel** – likes food tech best (wants to work in a restaurant). Dislikes drama (is not confident and classes make him uncomfortable). **Paula** – likes science (it is logical and interesting). Dislikes languages (they are hard and she can't pronounce French). **David** – loves languages (wants to work in tourism). Dislikes music (sings badly).*

> **!** **y → e**
>
> Notice in question 1 that Paula said that sciences are '**lógicas e interesantes**'. When the word **y** (*and*) is followed by a word that starts with an **i** or **hi**, then **y** changes to **e**:
>
> *big and important* → **grande e importante**   *sons and daughters* → **hijos e hijas**

2. Listen to these students (2.1–2.4) saying why they like their favourite subjects. What reason do they give? Write the correct letter.   TRACK 17

A	clear explanations	D	no homework
B	finds it easy	E	subject is fascinating
C	group work	F	varied activities

2.1 C   2.2 A   2.3 D   2.4 F

3. Talk about the subjects you like and dislike using the grid below for ideas.

Me gusta(n)	mucho / bastante	el ... la ... los ... las ... + *school subject*	porque	es / son	
No me gusta(n)	mucho / nada			el trabajo en grupo es	Me gusta(n)
Me encanta(n)				las clases / actividades son	
				no hay deberes.	
				el profesor / la profesora	Me gusta(n)
Detesto Odio Prefiero		al profesor de + *school subject* a la profesora de + *school subject*		(no) nos ayuda mucho. (no) explica muy bien. (no) es muy paciente.	
				es simpático(a) / antipático(a) / trabajador(a).	

> **!** Be careful when you use the verbs in column 1. Use **me** with **gustar** and **encantar** (**me gusta / me encanta**) but never with **prefiero**. (That would mean 'I prefer myself'!)

SCHOOL FACILITIES AND UNIFORM

¿Cómo es tu instituto?   *What is your school like?*

1. Read this description of Andrea's school and find the Spanish for the words and phrases below.

> Mi instituto está en las afueras del pueblo. El edificio no es muy nuevo, pero está limpio y bien decorado. Tenemos un gran gimnasio para las clases de educación física y un campo de deportes también. Por dentro, cuando entras, tienes la recepción a la izquierda y la sala de profesores a la derecha. La biblioteca tiene mesas para estudiar y varios ordenadores además de todos los libros. Hay muchas aulas para todas las asignaturas, incluyendo laboratorios de ciencias con todo el equipo necesario y salas de informática. En el recreo casi todos compran un bocadillo en la cafetería y luego salen al patio o juegan al baloncesto en las canchas.

1.1 gym / sports hall	1.4 library	1.7 classrooms	1.10 IT rooms
1.2 playing field	1.5 tables / desks	1.8 laboratories	1.11 yard
1.3 reception	1.6 computers	1.9 equipment	1.12 courts

2. Read the text again and complete the following sentences. Select the correct option.

   2.1 Andrea's school is **old and shabby / modern and bright / clean and in good condition**.

   2.2 On the right, when you go in, you will see the **staffroom / reception / library**.

   2.3 The science labs are **short of resources / well equipped / in a separate building**.

   2.4 To get a snack, most students **bring something from home / go to the shop next door / use the school cafeteria**.

   2.5 During break, students tend to **stay in the classroom / go outside / go on the computers**.

---

1. 1.1 *gimnasio*   1.2 *campo de deportes*   1.3 *recepción*   1.4 *biblioteca*   1.5 *mesas*
    1.6 *ordenadores*   1.7 *aulas*   1.8 *laboratorios*   1.9 *equipo*   1.10 *salas de informática*
    1.11 *patio*   1.12 *canchas*

2. 2.1 *clean and in good condition*   2.2 *staffroom*   2.3 *well equipped*
    2.4 *use the school cafeteria*   2.5 *go outside*

---

3. Using Andrea's description as a model, write a paragraph to describe your own school.

El uniforme   *(School) uniform*

Vocabulary

el pantalón	*trousers*	negro/a	*black*	
la falda	*skirt*	blanco/a	*white*	
la camisa	*shirt*	verde	*green*	
la chaqueta	*jacket / blazer*	amarillo/a	*yellow*	
la corbata	*tie*	gris	*grey*	
los calcetines	*socks*	azul	*blue*	
los zapatos	*shoes*	rojo/a	*red*	
de rayas	*striped / with stripes*	marrón	*brown*	

+ Remember

Remember the agreement pattern for adjectives:

rojo (m. sing), **roja** (f. sing), **rojos** (m. pl), **rojas** (f. pl)   **azul** (m/f. sing), **azules** (m/f. pl)

marrón loses the accent in the plural.

---

4. Complete this description of the uniforms in the picture, remembering to make the adjectives agree.

Los estudiantes llevan el pantalón (4.1) _____ o una falda (4.2) _____ y

los zapatos (4.3) _____ . La chaqueta del instituto es (4.4) _____ y

todos llevan la camisa (4.5) _____ . Los calcetines tienen que ser (4.6) _____ .

Llevan la corbata de rayas (4.7) v_____ y (4.8) a_____ .

4.1 gris   4.2 gris   4.3 negros   4.4 verde   4.5 blanca   4.6 negros   4.7 verdes   4.8 amarillas

---

5. Listen to these students (5.1–5.4) talking about their uniform.
Complete the grid for each student with adjectives in English.

 TRACK 18

	Trousers / skirt	Shirt	Jacket / blazer	Tie	Opinion
5.1					
5.2					
5.3					
5.4					

5.1 black / blue / grey / red and grey stripes / not bad   5.2 grey / white / red / black and blue stripes / not comfortable   5.3 blue / grey / blue / red / not practical
5.4 black / white / brown / brown and yellow stripes / ugly

SCHOOL LIFE

1. ⊕ Match the questions (1.1–1.8) to the correct statements (A–F).
   You will not need all the questions.

A. *Son muy trabajadores y nos ayudan mucho. Algunos son estrictos y nos dan demasiados deberes.*

B. *Hay bastante presión para sacar buenas notas y sentimos el estrés. Hay pocos casos de acoso, afortunadamente.*

C. *Escuchamos la explicación del profesor, hacemos ejercicios, hay trabajo en grupo y debates.*

D. *Salimos al patio y charlamos un rato. A veces tomamos un bocadillo y un café.*

E. *Hay que respetar el edificio y a todos los miembros del colegio. Tenemos que tener el equipo correcto y asistir a clase puntualmente.*

F. *Empezamos a las ocho y hay tres clases antes del recreo. Después hay tres clases más y terminamos a las dos y media.*

1.1 ¿Cómo es el horario de un día escolar típico?

1.2 ¿Qué es lo malo de tu instituto?

1.3 ¿Qué hacéis en una clase típica?

1.4 ¿Hay actividades y clubs después de las clases?

1.5 ¿Qué piensas de los profesores?

1.6 ¿Qué tipo de reglas hay en el colegio?

1.7 ¿Qué tal las comidas en el instituto?

1.8 ¿Qué hacéis durante el recreo?

1.1 F   1.2 B   1.3 C   1.5 A   1.6 E   1.8 D   Questions 1.4 and 1.7 are not needed.

2. ⊕ Using the vocabulary from this page, translate these sentences into **Spanish**.

2.1 On Tuesdays, we finish at half past three.

2.2 Occasionally, there are cases of bullying.

2.3 Sometimes, we chat in the yard.

2.4 Some teachers are very strict.

2.5 Generally, the rules are practical.

2.6 I get good marks in my homework.

2.1 Los martes, terminamos a las tres y media.

2.2 De vez en cuando, hay casos de acoso.

2.3 A veces, charlamos en el patio.

2.4 Algunos profesores son muy estrictos.

2.5 Generalmente, las reglas son prácticas.

2.6 Saco buenas notas en mis deberes.

➕ Remember

Note these useful expressions of time:

normalmente
normally / usually

generalmente
generally

de vez en cuando
occasionally

los martes
on Tuesdays

3. Listen to these students (3.1–3.4) talking about school. Which aspect of school is good and which is bad, according to each one?

TRACK 19

			Good	Bad
A	behaviour			
B	class activities	**3.1**		
C	exam results	**3.2**		
D	facilities	**3.3**		
E	rules	**3.4**		
F	teachers			
G	timetables			
H	uniform			

! Be careful – the opinions won't always come in the order you expect (1st good, 2nd bad), so listen carefully to all of the recording.

3.1 Good D, Bad E   3.2 Good B, Bad A   3.3 Good F, Bad H   3.4 Good C, Bad G

4. Look back at the ideas and vocabulary on these two pages and prepare answers to questions 1.1–1.8 on **page 36**. Then play the recording, pausing after each question to give your answer.

TRACK 20

5. You are writing an article about education.

Write approximately **60 words** in **Spanish**.

You must write something about each bullet point.

Mention:

- what you think of your school
- some activities you are going to do in class next week.

Example answer:

Generalmente, me gusta mi instituto, aunque algunas de las clases en mis asignaturas menos favoritas son un poco aburridas. Tenemos instalaciones buenas y modernas y los profesores son bastante simpáticos.

La semana que viene, vamos a tener un debate en la clase de religión. Creo que va a ser muy interesante. En dibujo, vamos a visitar una exposición de arte moderno en la ciudad. No me gusta el arte moderno, pero me gustan las excursiones. (75 words)

This question in the exam will have three bullet points and require a 90-word answer. It will include a bullet point requiring past tenses, with examples on **pages 51** to **92**.

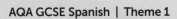

OPTIONS AT AGE 16

¿Qué puedes estudiar a los 16 años?   *What can you study at 16?*

1. ⓗ Read this article from a website on education and find the following expressions.

> Después de completar la enseñanza obligatoria, a los dieciséis años, los estudiantes españoles tienen la opción de continuar sus estudios en la educación secundaria. Pueden elegir diferentes especialidades académicas como ciencias, humanidades, arte o tecnología que les permitirán profundizar en las asignaturas que más les interesen. El programa, que se llama el Bachillerato, dura dos años y prepara a los estudiantes para acceder a la universidad.
>
> También existen otras opciones que los jóvenes pueden considerar, incluyendo programas de formación profesional en diferentes áreas, como cocina, informática, electrónica y mecánica entre otras. Estos ofrecen una formación más práctica y les da a los jóvenes las habilidades que necesitan para entrar en el mundo laboral.

1.1 to continue their studies   1.4 to get into university   1.7 the skills that they need

1.2 they can choose   1.5 vocational training courses   1.8 to go into the world of work

1.3 lasts two years   1.6 more practical training

profundizar en *to study in more depth*

1.1 continuar sus estudios   1.2 pueden elegir   1.3 dura dos años   1.4 acceder a la universidad   1.5 programas de formación profesional   1.6 formación más práctica   1.7 las habilidades que necesitan   1.8 entrar en el mundo laboral

2. Now adapt the expressions you have just found to translate the sentences below.

2.1 I want to continue my studies.

2.2 I am going to choose three different subjects.

2.3 The course lasts two years.

2.4 I hope to get into university.

2.5 I am going to do a vocational training course.

2.6 The training on these courses is more practical.

2.7 Afterwards, I will have* the skills that I need to enter the world of work.

*tendré *I will have*

2.1 Quiero continuar mis estudios.   2.2 Voy a elegir tres asignaturas diferentes.   2.3 El programa dura dos años.   2.4 Espero acceder a la universidad.   2.5 Voy a hacer un programa de formación profesional.   2.6 La formación en estos programas es más práctica.   2.7 Después, tendré las habilidades que necesito para entrar en el mundo laboral.

The future tense

The verb **tendré** that you saw and used in the last activity is an irregular form of the future tense. To form the future tense for regular verbs, take the whole infinitive (**-ar**, **-er**, **-ir**) and add these endings:

I	→	-é	**e.g. continuaré** *I will continue*
you singular	→	-ás	**estudiarás** *you will study*
he / she / it	→	-á	**ofrecerá** *he / she / it will offer*
we	→	-emos	**leeremos** *we will read*
you plural	→	-éis	**elegiréis** *you will choose*
they	→	-án	**permitirán** *they will permit / allow*

 Note that the endings are the same for all verbs.

Irregular stems

tener → tendr-
hacer → har-
poder → podr-
poner → pondr-
habrá = *there will be*

---

3. Listen to these young people (3.1–3.4) talking about their plans for the future. Which statements are correct? Write **A**, **B** or **A + B**. TRACK 21

3.1 She is going to   **A** do a science course   **B** work in a restaurant.

3.2 He is going to do a   **A** computer studies academic course   **B** vocational course in IT.

3.3 She is going to   **A** do some more research   **B** consult her teachers.

3.4 He is going to   **A** stay on at school   **B** go to university.

3.1 A + B   3.2 B   3.3 A + B   3.4 A + B

---

4. Put the verbs in brackets into the correct form of the future tense.

4.1 Óscar _____ (hablar) con sus profesores para pedir consejo.

4.2 El programa _____ (ser) ideal para las habilidades que necesito.

4.3 Los estudiantes _____ (elegir) sus asignaturas el lunes.

4.4 Yo _____ (hacer) formación profesional en mecánica.

4.5 ¿Tú _____ (poder) estudiar las asignaturas que prefieres?

4.1 hablará   4.2 será   4.3 elegirán   4.4 haré   4.5 podrás

---

5. Read aloud the following passage and then play the recording to check your pronunciation. TRACK 22

El año que viene haré bachillerato en mi instituto. Voy a elegir ciencias porque me gustan las asignaturas y quiero estudiar química y física en la universidad. También espero trabajar los sábados para ganar un poco de dinero.

THE WORLD OF WORK

¿Qué tipo de trabajo te interesa? *What type of work interests you?*

1. 🄷 Read the statements below and answer the questions in **English**.

Estoy buscando información sobre varias carreras en este momento, pero las dos que más me apetecen son el trabajo de un abogado o de un periodista. Para los dos creo que necesitaré un título universitario. **Ana**

Lo más importante para mí es tener un trabajo seguro con un salario bueno. No me importa trabajar en una oficina o un banco, pero preferiría tener los fines de semana libres. **José**

Lo que yo busco es un trabajo variado. Me aburro fácilmente y no quiero estar haciendo las mismas cosas todos los días. También, me atrae la idea de viajar, preferiblemente a otros países. **Susana**

A mí me gusta más un trabajo práctico, no me interesan las asignaturas académicas. Me gustaría hacer trabajo físico, por ejemplo trabajando en la construcción o al aire libre como en parques y jardines. **Alex**

1.1 What research is Ana currently doing?
1.2 What qualification does Ana need?
1.3 What is most important for José?
1.4 What does he say he would prefer?

1.5 What does Susana not want in a job? Why?
1.6 What other aspect appeals to her?
1.7 What two adjectives describe the work Alex wants?
1.8 What two options does Alex suggest?

> **la carrera** *career / university course*   **abogado** *lawyer*   **periodista** *journalist*
> **el título** *degree*   **seguro** *secure*   **el salario** *wage / salary*   **variado** *varied*
> **aburrirse** *to get bored*   **me apetece** *I fancy*   **al aire libre** *outdoors*

1.1 She is looking up information on several careers / courses.   1.2 a university degree
1.3 a secure job with a good wage / salary   1.4 his weekends free   1.5 She doesn't want to be doing the same thing every day because she gets bored easily.   1.6 travel, especially abroad
1.7 practical and physical   1.8 construction / building or outdoor work (in parks and gardens)

! Use **lo** + adjective to say 'the ... thing'.

e.g. **lo bueno** → *the good thing*   **lo mejor de ...** → *the best thing about ...*

lo malo → *the bad thing*   **lo peor de ...** → *the worst thing about ...*

lo que → *what* (when not asking a question)   **Lo que yo busco es ...** *What I'm looking for is ...*

2. Read the pros and cons and match them to the correct job.

2.1	➕ vacaciones largas ➖ mucha preparación	**A** Doctor
2.2	➕ comidas gratuitas ➖ clientes desagradables	**B** Postal worker
2.3	➕ descuentos en la tienda ➖ todo el día de pie	**C** Teacher
2.4	➕ mucho ejercicio ➖ perros agresivos	**D** Shop assistant
2.5	➕ ayudar a la gente ➖ muchos años de estudio	**E** Waiter / waitress

2.1 C   2.2 E   2.3 D   2.4 B   2.5 A

---

3. ❿ Listen to these people (3.1–3.4). Which job does each one do? Select the correct letter.

TRACK 23

Person 3.1 is **A** an insurance clerk   **B** a bank manager   **C** a counsellor
Person 3.2 is **A** a doctor   **B** a hospital receptionist   **C** a nurse
Person 3.3 is **A** an actor   **B** a film director   **C** a screenwriter
Person 3.4 is **A** a portrait painter   **B** a hairdresser   **C** a fashion designer

3.1 B   3.2 C   3.3 A   3.4 B

---

4. ❿ Translate this passage into **English**.

Creo que me gustaría ser técnico informático en una gran empresa. Me encanta usar los ordenadores y aprender sobre cómo funcionan. Sería genial poder ayudar a la gente con sus dificultades técnicas y explicar cómo arreglar el problema. Lo bueno es que hay muchos trabajos en este sector.

I think I would like to be an IT technician in a large company.
I love using computers and learning about how they work.
It would be great to be able to help people with their
technical difficulties and explain how to fix the problem.
The good thing is that there are lots of jobs in
this sector.

PREPARING FOR WORK

Buscando trabajo   *Looking for work*

1. Read these three adverts and decide which of the following requirements they each mention.

A

Infocom Tarragona

Ponte en contacto con nosotros si:

- tienes experiencia en negocios
- hablas inglés y español
- estás dispuesto a viajar con el trabajo
- eres una persona independiente y con iniciativa

B

Vacante laboral con
Hoteles Rocamar

¿Eres esta persona?

- tranquila y organizada
- capaz de trabajar bajo presión
- dispuesta a trabajar los fines de semana
- te relacionas bien con la gente

Busca más información en nuestro sitio web.

C

Arquitectos Sanz
busca ayudante

Requisitos

- un interés en diseño
- buenos conocimientos informáticos
- capaz de trabajar en equipo
- actitud positiva y creativa

1.1 can work weekends	1.5 able to work under pressure	1.9 creative
1.2 good IT knowledge	1.6 willing to travel	1.10 shows initiative
1.3 business experience	1.7 organised and calm	1.11 gets on with people
1.4 able to work in a team	1.8 speaks English	1.12 interested in design

A: 1.3, 1.6, 1.8, 1.10   B: 1.1, 1.5, 1.7, 1.11   C: 1.2, 1.4, 1.9, 1.12

2. You are asked these questions in an interview. Use the ideas and some of the expressions above to plan your answers.

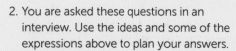

TRACK 24

When you are ready, play the recording and pause it after each question to give yourself time to reply. (Your answers don't have to be entirely true!)

2.1 ¿Qué tipo de personalidad tienes?

2.2 ¿Por qué piensas que eres la persona ideal para el trabajo?

2.3 ¿Cómo te llevas con la gente?

2.4 ¿Qué idiomas hablas?

2.5 ¿Qué experiencia tienes?

3. **H** Valeria has an interview. Her friends message her with advice.

Who gives these pieces of advice? Answer the questions using the initial of the friend.

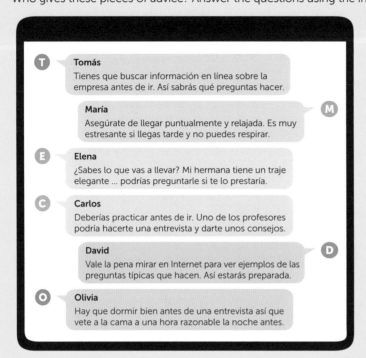

T Tomás
Tienes que buscar información en línea sobre la empresa antes de ir. Así sabrás qué preguntas hacer.

María M
Asegúrate de llegar puntualmente y relajada. Es muy estresante si llegas tarde y no puedes respirar.

E Elena
¿Sabes lo que vas a llevar? Mi hermana tiene un traje elegante ... podrías preguntarle si te lo prestaría.

C Carlos
Deberías practicar antes de ir. Uno de los profesores podría hacerte una entrevista y darte unos consejos.

David D
Vale la pena mirar en Internet para ver ejemplos de las preguntas típicas que hacen. Así estarás preparada.

O Olivia
Hay que dormir bien antes de una entrevista así que vete a la cama a una hora razonable la noche antes.

3.1 Dress smartly.

3.2 Get there with time to spare.

3.3 Research the company.

3.4 Have a practice interview.

3.5 Go to bed early the night before.

3.6 Prepare some questions to ask.

3.7 Think about what they could ask you.

3.8 Ask for a teacher's help.

3.9 Ensure you are calm and unhurried.

3.10 My sister might be able to help.

3.1 E   3.2 M   3.3 T   3.4 C   3.5 O   3.6 T   3.7 D   3.8 C   3.9 M   3.10 E

---

4. **H** Translate these sentences into **Spanish**.

4.1 You have to ask questions about the company.

4.2 Make sure to wear smart clothes.

4.3 You should sleep well the night before.

4.4 You could prepare some answers.

4.5 It's worthwhile looking at the company's website.

4.6 You must be prepared and relaxed.

4.1 Tienes que hacer preguntas sobre la empresa.

4.2 Asegúrate de llevar ropa elegante.

4.3 Deberías dormir bien la noche antes.

4.4 Podrías preparar unas / algunas preguntas.

4.5 Vale la pena mirar el sitio web de la empresa.

4.6 Hay que estar preparado y relajado.

! Notice these useful expressions in the text messages. They are all followed by an infinitive.

tienes que → *you have to*

asegúrate de → *make sure to*

deberías → *you should*

vale la pena → *it's worthwhile*

podrías → *you could*

hay que → *you must / one must*

EDUCATION AND WORK

Ponerlo todo junto · *Putting it all together*

1. Mateo has moved house and is about to start a new school. He emails his friend.
   Read the text and answer the questions in **English**.

   > ¡Hola Rodrigo!
   >
   > Ayer visité mi nuevo instituto para ver qué tal. Las clases empiezan el lunes que viene, pero me invitaron a ver el edificio y a conocer a algunos de los profesores. Es mucho más grande que mi colegio anterior – creo que me perderé de vez en cuando – pero es moderno y parece limpio y bien equipado. Lo bueno es que no está lejos de la casa nueva, así que será fácil ir andando por la mañana. Los profesores parecían agradables por lo general, aparte de la profe de historia que tenía una cara muy seria. Sin duda va a ser muy estricta. Para mí, lo peor será no conocer a ninguno de los otros estudiantes. Creo que me sentiré bastante incómodo al principio.
   >
   > Mateo

   1.1 When does the new term start?
   1.2 Why was he invited into school?
   1.3 Why does the size of the school worry him?
   1.4 What **three** things did he notice about the school building?
   1.5 How will he get to school and why?
   1.6 What was his impression of most of the teachers?
   1.7 What did he think about the history teacher?
   1.8 What does Mateo say is the worst thing about starting a new school?
   1.9 Look at the last line. What do you think **incómodo** means?

   A confident   **B** bullied   **C** uncomfortable

   1.1 Next Monday. 1.2 To see the building and meet some teachers. 1.3 He thinks he'll get lost.
   1.4 It's modern, clean and well equipped. 1.5 He'll walk; it's not far from his house.
   1.6 They're pleasant. 1.7 She has a serious face and will be strict. 1.8 Not knowing any other
   students. 1.9 C

2. Listen to these young people (2.1–2.4) talking about their current school. TRACK 25

   Are their opinions positive (**P**), negative (**N**) or both positive and negative (**P + N**)?

   2.1 P 2.2 N 2.3 P + N 2.4 P + N

Dictation

3. You will hear **five** sentences, repeated **three** times. Write them down in **Spanish**. (Note that on the Foundation **F** paper, there are only **four** sentences).

3.1 Tengo clases / de historia / y geografía.　*3.2 Las asignaturas / son difíciles / este año.*
3.3 El recreo / empieza / a las once.　*3.4 Me gustaría / ser médico / o enfermero.*
3.5 Quiero / cuidar a / otra gente.

4. **F** Complete each sentence with the correct word.

4.1 Me _____ mucho las ciencias.　(**A** gusta **B** gustan **C** gustaría)

4.2 El año próximo, _____ con mis estudios.　(**A** continuaré **B** continué **C** continuará)

4.3 Vale _____ prepararte bien para una entrevista.　(**A** el pan **B** la pena **C** lo peor)

4.4 Me encantan los _____, sobre todo el francés.　(**A** asignaturas **B** notas **C** idiomas)

4.5 Esta tarde, tengo _____ hacer mis deberes.　(**A** a **B** que **C** de)

4.1 B　4.2 A　4.3 B　4.4 C　4.5 B

Photo card

5. Look at the two photos and make notes about what you can say about them. Then set a timer and talk about the content of the photos.

Foundation **F** students have **one minute** to talk and Higher **H** students have a **minute and a half**. Listen to the recording to hear a student talking about the photos.

Photo 1　　　Photo 2

6. You are writing to a Spanish friend about school and your plans for next year. Write approximately **90 words** in **Spanish**. You must write something about each bullet point. Mention:
   - life at school
   - your favourite subject
   - what you plan to study next year

Example answer:
Estoy bastante contento/a en el instituto y me gustan la mayoría de las asignaturas, aparte de las matemáticas. Saco muy malas notas porque no entiendo las explicaciones, aunque la profesora es muy paciente conmigo. Mi clase favorita es la educación física porque parece que tengo talento en deportes. Me gusta el baloncesto, pero sobre todo el atletismo. El año que viene, voy a continuar con mis estudios en el instituto. Tenemos que elegir tres asignaturas y estudiaré educación física (¡claro!), con biología y psicología. Esta combinación será ideal para una carrera en deportes. *(93 words)*

KEY VOCABULARY

Students are expected to know 1200 items of vocabulary for Foundation tier and a further 500 for Higher tier. This list has some of the key vocabulary for Theme 1, but there are many more words listed in the AQA specification and in an interactive spreadsheet on the AQA website.

inglés / inglesa	English (nationality / adjective)
sacar buenas / malas notas	to get good / bad marks
el colegio	(secondary) school
los deberes	homework
el recreo	break (at school)
aprender	to learn
estudiar	to study
leer	to read
trabajar	to work
el profesor / la profesora	teacher (male / female)
el / la estudiante	student
el deporte	sport
enfermo	ill, sick
sano	healthy
vegetariano	vegetarian
estar en forma	to be fit
la dieta	diet
la salud	health
el estrés	stress
beber	to drink
comer	to eat
descansar	to rest, relax
español / española	Spanish
gracioso	funny
guapo	good-looking
joven	young
pequeño	little, small
simpático	nice, friendly
el hermano / la hermana	brother / sister
el padre	father
la madre	mother
el hombre	man
la mujer	woman
el matrimonio	marriage

EXAMINATION PRACTICE

People and lifestyle – Reading

🄗 You read a blog about family life on a Spanish website.

> Yo creo que las relaciones entre los padres y los hijos hoy son muy distintas de cómo eran para la generación anterior. Me parece que los padres tienen una actitud más relajada y menos estricta y casi se comportan como amigos, o quizá hermanos mayores. Los jóvenes tienen más libertad en su vida social. El mayor problema para los jóvenes de hoy es que tienen que depender de sus padres económicamente durante muchos años. Muchos viven en la casa familiar hasta que tienen treinta años o más.

Complete these sentences. Write the letter for the correct option.   [4 marks]

01 Parent–child relationships
  A   are difficult because of the generation gap   **B** have changed in recent years
  C   are not so different from how they used to be.

02 These days parents
  A   are more easy-going   **B** work longer hours   **C** choose to have fewer children.

03 Young people generally
  A   are well disciplined   **B** have more freedom   **C** respect their parents.

04 Many young people
  A   start a family at a later age   **B** look for a house to share   **C** stay at home for several years.

You see an online forum. Some Spanish students are discussing their lifestyle.

Martina
Nunca tengo hambre por la mañana y evito tomar el desayuno aunque mi madre me grita. Siempre llevo una manzana y una naranja al colegio para comer durante el recreo. Voy al colegio a pie y tardo media hora, así que hago bastante ejercicio simplemente yendo y volviendo del instituto.

Gael
No me gusta levantarme por la mañana y normalmente solo tengo tiempo para vestirme y salir. Durante el recreo compro un bocadillo y una botella de agua de la cafetería en el instituto. Soy muy deportista y juego en varios equipos, además de practicar la natación e ir al colegio en bici.

Who mentions the following? Write **M** for Martina, **G** for Gael or **M + G** for Martina and Gael.   [6 marks]

05   How they get to school   07   Eating fruit   09   Doing a lot of walking

06   Skipping breakfast   08   Having a sandwich   10   Going swimming

---

11   Translate the following sentences into **English**.   [4 marks]
  11.1   Tengo mucha suerte de tener un amigo como Martín.
  11.2   Es muy comprensivo y puedo confiar en él.

People and lifestyle – Listening

01–06 You are listening to the presenters on Spanish breakfast TV announcing what is on the show. Which feature of the programme do they each mention? Write the correct letter for each presenter (01–06). [6 marks]

TRACK 28

Presenter 01 _____

Presenter 02 _____

Presenter 03 _____

Presenter 04 _____

Presenter 05 _____

Presenter 06 _____

A	Choosing your options
B	Cooking vegan food
C	Exercising with friends
D	Friendship award
E	Keep fit for the elderly
F	Local job opportunities
G	Study support online
H	Solving sleep problems

---

❶ Listen to Isabel talking to her grandmother on the phone and telling her about her studies. Complete the sentences in English. [5 marks]

TRACK 29

07 Isabel says that, last year, religious studies _____ .

08 If they didn't do PE in school, _____ .

09 The literature teacher gives them _____ .

10 The Galicia trip offers a programme of _____ and _____ .

❶ Dictation

11–15 You will now hear **five** short sentences.

TRACK 30

Listen carefully and, using your knowledge of Spanish sounds, write down in **Spanish** exactly what you hear for each sentence.

You will hear each sentence **three** times: the first time as a full sentence, the second time in short sections and the third time again as a full sentence.

Use your knowledge of Spanish sounds and grammar to make sure that what you have written makes sense. Check carefully that your spelling is accurate. [10 marks]

(Note that, on the Foundation paper, there are only four sentences.)

People and lifestyle – Speaking

Role play

Plan what you are going to say in this role play, taking into account the number of details you will need. Remember to use a verb in each response.

Then play the recording, pausing after each question or statement so you can give your response. (**F** This is in the style of a Foundation tier role play).
When you see this **– ? –** you will have to ask a question.

TRACK 31

You are talking to your Venezuelan friend.

01 Say what your best friend looks like. (Give **one** detail.)

02 Say why you get on with your friend. (Give **one** detail.)

03 Say what you think of your school. (Give **one** opinion.)

04 Say what your favourite subject is. (Give **one** detail.)

? 05 Ask your friend a question about their family.

[10 marks]

06 **H Read aloud** the following passage and then answer the questions in the recording.
This is a Higher-tier task. [5 + 10 marks]

> Para tener una dieta equilibrada, yo debería comer menos carne roja, pero es muy difícil porque me encantan las hamburguesas. Hoy mi padre prepara pollo con verduras que es un plato muy saludable. Mi instituto organiza una campaña de ejercicio este jueves y voy a ir al colegio a pie.

TRACK 32

Photo card

07 Look at the two photos and prepare ideas on what to say about them. Remember to say something about both photos and to talk for one minute **F** or one and a half minutes **H**. [5 marks]

Photo 1

Photo 2

TRACK 33

08 Now answer the recorded questions for the unprepared conversation on the theme. [20 marks]

People and lifestyle – Writing

01 **F** Your Colombian friends asks you about your school.
Write an email to him.

Mention:

- teachers
- favourite subject
- facilities
- food
- break time.

[10 marks]

02 Translate the following sentences into **Spanish**.

[10 marks]

02.1 She has fair hair and she wears glasses.

02.2 Sometimes I fight with my younger brother.

02.3 I will continue with my studies next year.

02.4 The good thing is that I do not have to study IT.

02.5 I hate our uniform – it is very ugly.

03 You are writing an article about healthy lifestyle. Write approximately **90 words** in **Spanish**.
You must write something about each bullet point.

Mention:

- some healthy meals that you like
- the exercise you will do next week
- something healthy that you did last week.

[15 marks]

You have not revised the preterite tense in this guide yet, but there will always be a past tense in the writing paper.
Check out the preterite tense on **pages 54 and 150**

04 **H** You are writing a post for an online magazine about education and work.
Write approximately **150 words** in **Spanish**.
You must write something about each bullet point.

Mention:

- a typical day in your school
- your plans for education and work in the future.

[25 marks]

TOPICS FOR THEME 2
Popular culture

Specification coverage

Topic 1   Free-time activities
Topic 2   Customs, festivals and celebrations
Topic 3   Celebrity culture

Information about the four papers for Foundation ⒻF and Higher ⒽH tiers:

Paper 1 – Listening

Written exam:
35 minutes Ⓕ, 45 minutes Ⓗ
40 marks Ⓕ, 50 marks Ⓗ
25% of GCSE

The recording is controlled by the invigilator with built-in repetitions and pauses.

Each exam includes 5 minutes' reading time at the start of the question paper before the listening material is played and 2 minutes at the end of the recording to check your work.

Section A – Listening comprehension questions in English, to be answered in English or non-verbally (Ⓕ 32 marks, Ⓗ 40 marks).

Section B – Dictation where students transcribe 4 sentences (Ⓕ 8 marks) or 5 sentences (Ⓗ 10 marks).

Paper 2 – Speaking

Non-exam assessment (NEA):
7–9 minutes Ⓕ or 10–12 minutes Ⓗ +
15 minutes' supervised preparation time
50 marks, 25% of GCSE

Role play – 10 marks, 1-1.5 minutes. Ⓕ Ⓗ

Reading aloud passage and short conversation – 15 marks.
Recommended time 2-2.5 minutes Ⓕ and 3-3.5 minutes Ⓗ.
Minimum 35 words Ⓕ and minimum 50 words Ⓗ.

Photo card discussion (two photos) – 25 marks.
Photo card discussion time:
4-5 minutes Ⓕ and 6-7 minutes Ⓗ.

Paper 4 – Writing

Written exam: 1 hour 10 minutes Ⓕ,
1 hour 15 minutes Ⓗ
50 marks, 25% of GCSE

Set of three short writing tasks. Ⓕ only.
25 marks.

Translation of sentences from English into Spanish, minimum 35 words Ⓕ, or 50 words Ⓗ (10 marks).

Produce a piece of writing in response to three compulsory bullet points, approximately 90 words in total. Choose from two questions (15 marks). Ⓕ Ⓗ

Open-ended writing task.
Two compulsory bullet points, approximately 150 words in total. Choose from two questions. (25 marks). Ⓗ only.

Paper 3 – Reading

Written exam: 45 minutes Ⓕ, 1 hour Ⓗ
50 marks, 25% of GCSE

Section A – Reading comprehension questions in English, to be answered in English or non-verbally (40 marks).

Section B – Translation from Spanish into English, minimum of 35 words Ⓕ or 50 words Ⓗ (10 marks).

ACTIVITIES AT HOME

¿Qué te gusta hacer en casa? — *What do you like doing at home?*

Useful vocabulary

leer revistas	*to read magazines*	ver películas	*to watch films*
descansar	*to rest*	jugar videojuegos	*to play video games*
escuchar música	*to listen to music*	navegar por Internet	*to surf the Internet*
tocar la guitarra	*to play the guitar*	cocinar	*to cook*
grabar vídeos	*to record videos*	chatear	*to chat (online)*

Talking about what you are doing – the present continuous

When you talk about what you 'are doing', you need the present continuous.

To form it, you use the verb **estar** + the present participle.

estoy
estás
está   **+**   **-ar** verbs: remove the **-ar** and add **-ando**
estamos
estáis   **-er/-ir** verbs: remove the **-er** and add **-iendo**
están

Some present participles are irregular, e.g. **leer** (**estoy leyendo** *I am reading*) and **dormir**
(**ⓗ estoy durmiendo** *I am sleeping*).

1. Listen to María describing the activities of different members (1.1–1.5) of her family. Which family members is she talking about and what are they doing? Write the answer in **English**.

TRACK 34

   1.1 brother – chatting on WhatsApp / phone
   1.2 parents – cooking 1.3 grandmother –
   resting 1.4 sisters – watching a film
   1.5 María – reading a magazine article.

    It is very important to listen out for endings when identifying family members (e.g. **hermano** / **hermana**).

2. Put the verbs in brackets into the correct form of the present continuous tense.

   2.1 Yo _____ (jugar) videojuegos en línea.

   2.2 Mi hermano _____ (tocar) la guitarra en su dormitorio.

   2.3 Mis primos _____ (dormir) en sus camas.

   2.4 Mi mejor amiga y yo _____ (grabar) vídeos en el móvil.

   2.1 estoy jugando   2.2 está tocando   2.3 están durmiendo   2.4 estamos grabando

Adjectives to describe activities

agradable	pleasant	gratis	free
emocionante	exciting	interesante	interesting
educativo/a	educational	difícil	difficult
activo/a	active	caro/a	expensive
físico/a	physical	tranquilo/a	calm
social	social	sano/a	healthy
animado/a	lively	relajante	relaxing

3. Read Miguel's description of what his friends are doing and answer the questions.

A mis amigos y yo nos gusta hacer diferentes actividades en casa. Por ejemplo, mi amigo Paco está en su ordenador navegando por Internet porque le encanta buscar información sobre la historia ya que piensa que es muy educativa. Mi mejor amiga Inés está escuchando música porque le gusta estar tranquila y relajada. Cuando estoy de vacaciones normalmente paso tiempo jugando al fútbol, pero ahora no puedo porque estoy leyendo un libro para mi clase de inglés. Siempre que no puedo ver a mis amigos, paso el sábado chateando en línea. Ahora estoy hablando por WhatsApp en el chat de mi clase. Me encanta porque es gratis.

3.1 Why is Paco on the computer?

3.2 Why does Paco like history?

3.3 Why does Inés like to listen to music?

3.4 Why can't Miguel play football now?

3.5 What does Miguel do when he can't see his friends?

3.6 Why does Miguel like WhatsApp?

3.1 Because he loves looking for information (on history).   3.2 It's educational.
3.3 She likes to be calm and relaxed.   3.4 Because he is reading a book (for English).
3.5 He chats online.   3.6 It's free.

4. Read aloud this passage and then listen to the recording to check your pronunciation.

TRACK 35

Ayer pasé dos horas leyendo. Me encanta la lectura, pero prefiero las actividades más activas. Mi mejor amiga se llama Amaya y siempre que la llamo está durmiendo y viendo la tele. Es muy agradable, pero puede ser perezosa.

+ Remember

Remember that **y** (when followed by a vowel) and **ll** are pronounced exactly the same.

ACTIVITIES OUTSIDE THE HOME

Actividades con tus amigos | *Activities with your friends*

Useful vocabulary

 ganar un partido
to win a match

 ir a conciertos
to go to concerts

 jugar al baloncesto
to play basketball

 ir a una fiesta
to go to a party

 ir de compras
to go shopping

 ir al cine
to go to the cinema

 pasarlo bien / mal
to have a good / bad time

 bailar
to dance

 hacer ejercicio
to do exercise

 salir con (mis) amigos
to go out with (my) friends

 reírse
to laugh

 tomar el sol
to sunbathe

 ir de excursión
to go on a trip

 caminar
to walk

Talking about what you did – the preterite tense

See **page 150** for more details.

The preterite tense is used to describe what you did in the past and are no longer doing.

The regular endings for this tense are:

-ar verbs		-er / -ir verbs	
-é	bailé	-í	comí
-aste	bailaste	-iste	comiste
-ó	bailó	-ió	comió
-amos	bailamos	-imos	comimos
-asteis	bailasteis	-isteis	comisteis
-aron	bailaron	-ieron	comieron

! Accents are really important in this tense.

For example, **un baile** means 'a dance', but **bailé** means 'I danced'. **Bailo** means 'I dance', but **bailó** means 'he/she danced'.

1. Put the verbs in brackets into the correct form of the preterite tense.

> Durante las vacaciones de verano, **1.1** (pasar) mucho tiempo con mis amigos. Mi mejor amigo y yo **2.2** (salir) al centro de la ciudad y **1.3** (comprar) ropa. Por la tarde yo **1.4** (nadar) en la piscina del pueblo. Después de cenar, mis amigos **1.5** (bailar) en una fiesta, pero yo **1.6** (quedarse) en casa y **1.7** (ver) la televisión.

1.1 pasé   1.2 salimos   1.3 compramos   1.4 nadé   1.5 bailaron   1.6 me quedé   1.7 vi

¿Qué hiciste? *What did you do?*

The preterite tense - irregular verbs

The preterite tense is the most irregular one in Spanish. Some of the most common irregular verbs in the preterite are:

ir → fui, fuiste, fue, fuimos, fuisteis, fueron

hacer → hice, hiciste, hizo ...

dar → di, diste, dio, dimos, disteis, dieron

tener → tuve, tuviste, tuvo ...

H Other verbs need to change their spelling slightly to maintain the sound in the stem.

jugar → jugué, jugaste ...   tocar → toqué, tocaste ...   empezar → empecé, empezaste, ...

2. **H** Translate these sentences into **Spanish**.

2.1 Last year, I went to the beach in my holidays.

2.2 I walked with my dog this morning.

2.3 Two years ago, my sister went on a trip with school.

2.4 My friends went to the cinema last Saturday.

2.5 I played guitar in a concert last week.

2.1 El año pasado, fui a la playa en mis vacaciones.   2.2 Caminé / Di un paseo / fui de paseo con mi perro esta mañana.   2.3 Hace dos años, mi hermana fue de excursión / hizo una excursión con el colegio.   2.4 Mis amigos fueron al cine el sábado pasado.   2.5 Toqué la guitarra en un concierto la semana pasada.

Photo card

3. Look at the two photos and make notes about what you can say about them. Then set a timer and talk about the content of the photos.

Foundation **F** students have **one minute** to talk and Higher **H** students have a **minute and a half**. Listen to the recording to hear a student talking about the photos.

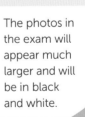

TRACK 36

Photo 1

Photo 2

! The photos in the exam will appear much larger and will be in black and white.

TV AND CINEMA

¿Qué prefieres ver? *What do you prefer to watch?*

1. Read about what these people like to watch and why. Look for these phrases in the texts.

> Me encanta ver telenovelas porque son muy entretenidas.

> No soporto los documentales: los encuentro muy aburridos, aunque son educativos.

> Lo que más me gusta es ir al cine y ver películas de dibujos animados.

> Me encanta ver el *resumen de los partidos de la semana en el programa de deportes.

> Los programas de cocina son relajantes y me ayudan a olvidarme del estrés.

> El protagonista de mi serie favorita es un actor fantástico y con mucho talento.

1.1 I find them	1.3 main character	1.5 they help me	1.7 what I like the most
1.2 relaxing	1.4 entertaining	1.6 I can't stand	1.8 a lot of talent

*resumen = summary

1.1 los encuentro   1.2 relajantes   1.3 protagonista   1.4 entretenidas   1.5 me ayudan (a)
1.6 no soporto   1.7 lo que más me gusta   1.8 mucho talento

＋ Remember

When talking or writing about films and TV, agreement is really important. Make sure that the verbs match their subjects and that adjectives agree with their nouns (see **page 10**).

Me encanta**n las** pelícu**las** de aventuras porque **son** emocionant**es**.

No soporto **los** program**as** de telerrealidad porque **son** repetiv**os**.

2. Translate these sentences into Spanish.

   2.1 I can't stand soap operas because they are not interesting.

   2.2 I love sports programmes because I find them lively.

   2.3 What I like the most is to watch reality TV programmes.

   2.4 Documentaries help me learn because they are educational.

2.1 No soporto las telenovelas porque no son interesantes.   2.2 Me encantan los programas de deporte(s) porque los encuentro animados.   2.3 Lo que más me gusta es ver programas de telerrealidad.   2.4 Los documentales me ayudan a aprender porque son educativos.

¿Con qué frecuencia vas al cine?   How often do you go to the cinema?

3. Match up the Spanish and the English for these frequency expressions.

3.1	a menudo		**A**	always
3.2	a veces		**B**	each day
3.3	cada día		**C**	every day
3.4	casi nunca		**D**	every now and then
3.5	de vez en cuando		**E**	hardly ever
3.6	dos veces al año		**F**	never
3.7	nunca		**G**	often
3.8	raramente		**H**	once a month
3.9	siempre		**I**	rarely
3.10	todos los días		**J**	sometimes
3.11	una vez al mes		**K**	twice a year

3.1 G   3.2 J   3.3 B   3.4 E   3.5 D   3.6 K   3.7 F   3.8 I   3.9 A   3.10 C   3.11 H

Role play

TRACK 37

4. 🅗 Plan what you are going to say in this role play, taking into account the number of details you will need. Then play the recording, pausing after each question or statement so you can give your response. (This is a Higher tier role play.)

4.1 Say what you do with your friends at the weekend. (Give **two** details.)

4.2 Give your opinion about going to the cinema and say why you think that. (Give **one opinion** and **one reason**.)

4.3 Say what you did at home last Saturday. (Give **two** details.)

4.4 Say when you like to listen to music.

? 4.5 Ask your friend a question about their free time.

5. Prepare **four** sentences, each describing an activity you do in your free time and how often you do it.

Learn them and say them from memory.

ACTIVITIES IN THE PRESENT, PAST AND FUTURE

In order to achieve higher marks in your speaking and writing, you need to demonstrate that you can use three different time frames.

Remember that time frame is not the same as tense – for example, even though the tense in **Espero ir a España** *I hope to go to Spain* is the present, the sentence expresses a future time frame.

Equally, **Toco la guitarra desde hace dos años** *I have been playing the guitar for two years* is a past time frame, even though the verb is in the present.

Using expressions like this, as well as a variety of tenses, can help you increase the complexity of your Spanish.

These are some useful time expressions you can use when writing a passage using three time frames.

Past	
hace dos años	two years ago
el fin de semana pasado	last weekend
en mis últimas vacaciones	on my last holiday
cuando era pequeño/a (+ imperfect)	when I was little

Present	
normalmente	normally
siempre	always
todos los fines de semana	every weekend
los domingos	on Sundays
por la mañana	in the morning

Future	
el año próximo	next year
el fin de semana que viene	next weekend
en mis próximas vacaciones	in / during my next holiday
dentro de cinco años	in five years' time
cuando sea mayor	when I am older
cuando tenga veinte años	when I am twenty years old
algún día	someday

The imperfect tense

The imperfect tense is used to describe things in the past, or to say what used to happen.

It is formed by removing the -ar/-er/-ir and adding the following endings:

	-ar	-er / -ir
I	aba	ía
you	abas	ías
he/she/it	aba	ía
we	ábamos	íamos
you pl	abais	íais
they	aban	ían

There are only 3 irregular verbs: ser, ir and ver. See **page 153**.

+ Remember

When writing a text using different tenses, it is good practice to flag up when you are changing from one tense to another by using one of these expressions.

1. ❶ Choose the correct option for the gap.
   This type of exercise appears in the Foundation writing exam only.

   1.1 El fin de semana próximo _____ con mis amigos.
   voy a salir   salí   salgo

   1.2 Todas las mañanas _____ a las siete.
   me levanté   me levanto   se levantó

   1.3 Algún día _____ una casa enorme.
   compraré   compré   compro

   1.4 Cuando voy al colegio siempre _____ mi uniforme.
   llevaré   llevé   llevo

2. Put the verbs in brackets into the correct **yo** (I) form in the appropriate tense. Then translate the sentences into **English**.

   2.1 El fin de semana pasado _____ (comer) en un restaurante.

   2.2 Todos los fines de semana _____ (jugar) al baloncesto.

   2.3 Dentro de ocho años _____ (estudiar) en la universidad.

   2.4 Los domingos _____ (ver) la tele en casa.

   2.5 Hace dos años _____ (visitar) a mi amigo en el sur de España.

   2.6 Cuando sea mayor _____ (tocar) la guitarra en un grupo de música.

   2.7 En mis últimas vacaciones _____ (comprar) recuerdos en las tiendas locales.

   1.1 voy a salir   1.2 me levanto   1.3 compraré   1.4 llevo

   *2.1 comí – Last weekend I ate in a restaurant.   2.2 juego – Every weekend I play basketball.
   2.3 estudiaré – In eight years' time I will study at university.   2.4 veo – On Sundays I watch TV at home.   2.5 visité – Two years ago I visited my friend in the south of Spain.   2.6 tocaré – When I am older, I will play the guitar in a music band.   2.7 compré – On my last holiday I bought souvenirs in the local shops.*

Dictation

3. Listen to these five sentences and write them down in **Spanish**. You will hear them once in full, a second time in sections, and once again in full the third time through.

   TRACK 38

   *3.1 El año pasado / jugué al fútbol / en un equipo.   3.2 Me gusta grabar / vídeos en el jardín.
   3.3 Encuentro los documentales / demasiado monótonos.
   3.4 Dar un paseo / es bueno / para la salud.   3.5 No aguanto / las películas marciales.*

WHAT OTHER PEOPLE DO

¿Qué hace tu familia? **What do your family do?**

To add complexity to your writing, try to include some verbs in other persons. For example, do not just write about what you did last weekend in your free time, also include in your answer what your friends did.

Another way of adding complexity is introducing some irregular verbs.

1. Read these comments describing what people do, did or will do in their free time.

"Cuando *era* pequeño, mi hermano siempre *iba* al parque a jugar al fútbol con sus amigos, pero yo prefería quedarme en casa. Ahora practico más deporte."

Esteban

"Dentro de dos semanas, mis primos *saldrán* al cine y después a un restaurante para celebrar el cumpleaños de mi tía. Creo que *podrán* pasarlo bien porque les encanta la comida japonesa."

Inés

"Siempre que *estoy* en casa, *juego* con mi ordenador. A veces mis hermanos *tienen* que ayudarme con mis deberes, especialmente matemáticas y ciencias, que *son* mis peores asignaturas."

Javier

"El sábado pasado, *fuimos* al centro comercial para comprar el uniforme para el colegio. Mi padre y yo *estuvimos* allí tres horas. *Hizo* bastante calor, así que decidimos ir a la cafetería cuando acabamos."

Alicia

H The verbs highlighted in above are all irregular verbs in different tenses. For each of them, write down the tense, the infinitive form and the meaning of the infinitive form.

era – imperfect, ser, to be   iba – imperfect, ir, to go   saldrán – future, salir, to go out podrán – future, poder, to be able to   estoy – present, estar, to be   juego – present, jugar, to play   tienen – present, tener, to have   son – present, ser, to be   fuimos – preterite, ir, to go estuvimos – preterite, estar, to be   hizo – preterite, hacer, to do / make (in this context – to be + weather)

2. Listen to these four people talking about their free time. Are they talking about the present (**N** – now), the past (**P**) or the future (**F**)?

TRACK 39

2.1 N   2.2 P   2.3 F   2.4 N

3. Prepare answers for these questions. Use some of the verbs highlighted on the previous page in your answers, in different persons.

The questions have been translated to help you.

1. ¿Dónde fuisteis tu familia y tú el fin de semana pasado?
   Where did you and your family go last weekend?

2. ¿Qué hacías cuando eras pequeño/a?
   What did you used to do when you were little?

3. ¿Dónde saldrás con tus amigos la semana que viene?
   Where will you go out with your friends next week?

4. ¿Qué haces en casa los domingos?
   What do you do at home on Sundays?

4. This student has written roughly **75 words** about a weekend that was not enjoyable in answer to the second bullet point of this Higher writing task.
The full task requires **150 words**. Mention:

- your favourite activities to do at home
- a recent weekend that you did not enjoy.

El fin de semana, no lo pasé nada bien. Mis amigos y yo **fuimos** *al centro comercial, pero mi tienda de deportes favorita* **estaba** *cerrada.* **Fuimos** *al cine para ver la última película de James Bond, pero ya no* **estaba***, así que* **tuvimos** *que ver una película romántica, que mi amigo* **detestó***. El fin de semana próximo* preferiría *ir al centro de la ciudad para ir de compras. Espero que lo* **pasaremos** *mejor.*

! Notice how, in answering the bullet point, another two tenses are introduced (underlined) to increase variety and complexity. Also, there are some verbs using different persons of the verb other than 'I' (in bold). (See **page 82**.) Now it's your turn to have a go at the above task. **Write approximately 150 words, and remember to write something about both bullet points.**

FREE-TIME ACTIVITIES

Ponerlo todo junto   *Putting it all together*

1. Read what Miguel, José and Inma say about their free time.
   Match the correct person with each of the following questions.

   > Cuando no tengo nada que hacer, me gusta pintar en mi dormitorio. El diseño es mi asignatura favorita. El año pasado, participé en un concurso de arte y gané el primer premio. Sin embargo, no soporto el deporte.

   Miguel

   > El verano pasado, pasé mucho tiempo en la playa. Me encanta practicar deportes acuáticos y también tomar el sol. El sábado, fui a una fiesta pero no lo pasé bien porque había demasiada gente.

   José

   > Me encantan los deportes de equipo y participo en competiciones con mi colegio todos los fines de semana. Cuando sea mayor, quisiera ser miembro del equipo de mi ciudad. Seré famosa y ganaré mucho dinero.

   Inma

   Write **M** for Miguel, **J** for José or **I** for Inma.

   1.1   Who would like to be famous in the future?

   1.2   Who does not like sport?

   1.3   Who did not enjoy themselves at the weekend?

   1.4   Who won a competition last year?

   1.1 I   1.2 M   1.3 J   1.4 M

Photo card

2. Look at the two photos and make notes about what you can say about them. Then set a timer and talk about the content of the photos.

   TRACK 40

   Foundation **F** students have **one minute** to talk and Higher **H** students have **one and a half minutes**. Then listen to the recording to hear an example of what could be said.

Photo 1   Photo 2

3. You are writing an article about free time.

Write approximately **90 words** in **Spanish**. You must write something about each point.

Mention:

- if you prefer team sports or individual sports
- what you did with your friends last weekend
- what you will do in your free time after you finish your exams.

Before having a go, take a look at the worked example below, then look back at the whole unit and write your own answer.

> This type of question appears in both Foundation and Higher papers.
> There is always a bullet point in the present, one in the past and one in the future. Remember to use a variety of verbs (including irregulars and verbs in different persons) and a variety of vocabulary and linking words.

Worked example

Linking word to present two contrasting ideas

Gives a reason for the opinion

More complex way of giving an example

Use of comparative

Shows good knowledge of an irregular imperfect

Complex opinion

Preterite tense, in first person plural

Idiomatic expression in the preterite tense

Time expressions to organise your writing

Aunque me gustan algunos deportes individuales, tales como la natación, porque son muy buenos para la salud, en general, prefiero los deportes de equipo. Me encanta jugar al baloncesto con mis amigos porque soy bastante bueno, y es más social que quedarse en casa.

El fin de semana pasado era mi cumpleaños, así que mis amigos y yo fuimos al cine para ver una película de acción. Creo que el cine es un poco caro pero vale la pena. Lo pasé genial.

Después de mis exámenes, primero me relajaré. Luego, voy a organizar una fiesta en mi casa que será muy divertida. **102 words**

Immediate future

Future tense, in two different persons

DAILY ROUTINES

¿Qué haces normalmente? *What do you normally do?*

Useful vocabulary

despertarse (ie)	*to wake up*	levantarse	*to get up*
ducharse	*to shower*	vestirse (i)	*to get dressed*
desayunar	*to have breakfast*	salir de casa	*to leave the house*
llegar al instituto	*to arrive at school*	volver a casa (ue)	*to go back home*
hacer los deberes	*to do homework*	relajarse	*to relax*
merendar (ie)	*to have a snack*	ver la tele	*to watch TV*
cenar	*to have dinner*	acostarse (ue)	*to go to bed*

1. Take a look at 'The basics' on **pages 2–4** to refresh numbers and telling the time, and then write these times in **Spanish**, making sure that you write the numbers out in full!

   1.1 It is 4.45.

   1.2 At 7.15.

   1.3 It is 1.10.

   1.4 At 10.50.

   1.5 It is 6.30.

   1.6 At 2.25.

1.1 Son las cinco menos cuarto.   1.2 A las siete y cuarto.   1.3 Es la una y diez.   1.4 A las once menos diez.   1.5 Son las seis y media.   1.6 A las dos y veinticinco.

+ Remember

Knowing your numbers can score you good marks in an exam. They can come up in ages, addresses, prices, telephone numbers, etc., so it pays to learn them.

Reflexive verbs

Most verbs that describe daily routines are reflexive: that means that they need an extra pronoun (**me**, **te**, **se**, etc.). Quite a few of them are also radical-changing verbs (look at the letters in brackets after some of them in the table on the previous page), so they can be quite challenging.
See **page 149** for more details.

levantarse	**vestirse**
me levanto	me visto
te levantas	te vistes
se levanta	se viste
nos levantamos	nos vestimos
os levantáis	os vestís
se levantan	se visten

Daily routine verbs are a good way of showing off your Spanish in the exam, especially if you are using a reflexive radical-changing verb in a person other than 'I'.

2. Samuel describes his daily routine.

   Write down what time he does each action.

   TRACK 41

   Gets up at 7.10, showers at 7.20, eats breakfast at 7.30, leaves home at 7.55, lessons start at 8.25, goes back home at 4.20, has a snack at 4.30, goes to bed at 10.30 or 10.45.

3. **H** Translate the following into **Spanish**.

   3.1 You get up.

   3.2 My brother showers.

   3.3 My sister has breakfast.

   3.4 My parents go to bed.

   3.5 I get dressed.

   3.6 You wake up.

   3.7 My sister and I have a snack.

   3.8 My friends go back home.

   3.1 Te levantas.
   3.2 Mi hermano se ducha.
   3.3 Mi hermana desayuna.
   3.4 Mis padres se acuestan.
   3.5 Me visto.
   3.6 Te despiertas.
   3.7 Mi hermana y yo merendamos.
   3.8 Mis amigos vuelven a casa.

1. Read these texts about two Spanish festivals and find the expressions in the texts.

En mis vacaciones, fui a la plaza de toros de Madrid, que se llama Las Ventas. Es la mayor del mundo. Aunque la corrida fue espectacular, y requiere mucho talento, no me gustó ver sufrir a los toros. El traje del **torero** es multicolor y muy caro de fabricar. La corrida es muy larga: dura unas dos horas. El problema es que estaba sentado al sol así que hizo muchísimo calor.

En julio en Pamplona se celebran los Sanfermines, en honor del santo patrón de la ciudad. Por la mañana temprano hay un **cohete** en el cielo muy ruidoso que anuncia el comienzo de la carrera. Cada carrera solo dura unos minutos. Me encantó el ambiente en la ciudad, pero yo nunca correría porque es demasiado peligroso.

1.1 bullring	1.4 I was sitting in the sun	1.7 lasts only a few minutes	1.10 the bullfight
1.2 bulls	1.5 I would never run	1.8 the atmosphere	1.11 patron saint
1.3 early in the morning	1.6 It's the biggest in the world.	1.9 the beginning	1.12 the race

2. Look at the two words in bold. There is one in each text.

   2.1 What is a **torero**?   **A** A person   **B** An animal   **C** An object

   2.2 What is a **cohete**?   **A** A party   **B** A drink   **C** A rocket

1.   1.1 plaza de toros   1.2. toros   1.3. Por la mañana temprano   1.4. estaba sentado al sol   1.5. nunca correría   1.6. Es la mayor del mundo.   1.7. solo dura unos minutos   1.8. el ambiente   1.9. el comienzo   1.10. la corrida   1.11. santo patrón   1.12. la carrera

2.   2.1 A – A person (a bullfighter)   2.2. C – A rocket (firework)

Talking about what you would do — the conditional

The conditional is formed like the future tense: the endings are added straight onto the infinitive verb (**-ar** / **-er** / **-ir**), without removing anything first.

The endings of er/ir verbs are the same as the imperfect → **ía**, **ías**, **ía**, **íamos**, **íais**, **ían**.

There are a few irregular verbs, which have the same stem changes as they do in the future.

Example

salir *to go out* → **saldré** *I will go out* (future) → **saldría** *I would go out* (conditional)

See **page 155** for more details.

 Remember

Remember that in your exam you need to use **three** time frames — the conditional is a 'future' time frame. You do not need a future tense if you have some conditionals, but it is a good idea to include both so that your writing and speaking show more variety of structure.

3. Read aloud this passage and then listen to the recording to check your pronunciation.

TRACK 42

> En mis próximas vacaciones, me gustaría ir al sur de España. Iría a una corrida de toros porque parece muy interesante. Sin embargo, creo que podría ser un poco triste ver a los toros sufrir. También, tendría que pasar mucho tiempo al sol. Sería demasiado caluroso.

4. Write approximately **75 words** about a festival you would like to visit.

   Make sure that you include some verbs in the conditional and the future tense.

   Look at the example below.

> *En abril, si puedo, iré al carnaval de Cádiz. Es una fiesta donde hay mucha música y mucho humor. Creo que sería fantástico porque los disfraces en los desfiles son espectaculares, y también podría ir al teatro para ver un espectáculo de grupos muy divertidos que cantan canciones graciosas. Me parece que será increíble disfrutar el ambiente en la ciudad. Además, la playa está muy cerca, así que podremos nadar en el mar.*
> **73 words**

MEXICAN FESTIVALS

El Día de Muertos   *The Day of the Dead*

Useful vocabulary

pasarlo bien / mal	*to have a good / bad time*	una canción	*a song*
los dulces	*sweets*	los fuegos artificiales	*fireworks*
una banda	*a music band*	el rey / la reina	*king / queen*
las Fallas	*Valencian celebration*	quemar	*to burn*
la estatua	*statue*	un desfile	*a parade*
un disfraz	*a costume*	el fuego	*fire*
llevar	*to wear*	el / un traje	*suit / costume*

Describing a photo

Look at the picture below of El Día de Muertos in Mexico, and at the discussion prompts.

- You could say where people are. (**Creo que es una foto del Día de Muertos en México.**)
- You could say what people are doing in the picture. (**Hay unas mujeres bailando en la calle, están sonriendo.**)
- You could talk about what people are wearing. The picture will be in black and white, but you could still guess what colour items are. (**Las mujeres llevan disfraces negros, con flores de muchos colores.**)
- You could talk about the physical appearance of the people in the picture, or even the weather. (**La mujer tiene el pelo negro y largo y los ojos marrones, hace sol y calor.**)
- You could make an educated guess as to what people are feeling. (**Creo que las mujeres están muy contentas porque el desfile es increíble.**)

1. Now look at the two pictures below and make notes on them. Practise saying your answer. If possible, you could record yourself. You need to talk for one minute **F** or one and a half minutes **H**. Then listen to the example answer.

TRACK 43

Photo 1

Photo 2

Using prepositions

Prepositions are small words that can often be overlooked but can play an important role in the content and accuracy of your Spanish.

Some of the most important ones to learn are:

con	with
a	to, at
contra	against
entre	between
sin	without
de	of
delante (de)	in front (of)
encima (de)	on / over

para	to / in order to / for
por	for / because of
sobre	over / above / about
según	according to
desde	from / since
en	in / on
detrás (de)	behind
debajo (de)	under

2. **❿** Fill in the gaps with **one** of the prepositions from the table above. Then translate the sentences into **English**.

2.1 Quiero ir al carnaval _____ mis amigos.

2.2 _____ mi padre, las corridas son muy crueles.

2.3 No he visitado las Fallas _____ que tenía cinco años.

2.4 No puedes ir de vacaciones a España _____ ver alguna fiesta en algún lugar.

2.5 En las corridas, un hombre lucha _____ un toro.

2.6 Me gustaría ir _____ Buñol _____ participar en la Tomatina (tomato festival).

2.7 El gato está escondido _____ de la mesa.

2.8 Estoy viendo una película _____ el Día de Muertos.

2.1 *con – I want to go to the carnival with my friends.*

2.2 *según – According to my dad, bullfights are very cruel.*

2.3 *desde – I haven't visited the Fallas since I was five.*

2.4 *sin – You can't go on holiday to Spain without seeing some festival somewhere.*

2.5 *con / contra – In bullfights, a man fights with / against a bull.*

2.6 *a, para – I would like to go to Buñol (in order) to take part in the tomato festival.*

2.7 *debajo / detrás – The cat is hidden under / behind the table.*

2.8 *sobre – I am watching a film about the Day of the Dead.*

CELEBRATIONS

¿Te gusta celebrar?   **Do you like celebrating?**

1. Read these texts about people's family celebrations.

¡Me encantan las bodas! El año pasado, fui a la boda de mi tío Nicolás y pasé una noche fantástica con toda mi familia.

Miguel

Mucha gente dice que lo mejor de las Navidades son los regalos, pero para mí, lo mejor es la cena de Nochebuena con todos tus familiares.

Andrés

Adoro recibir regalos para mi cumpleaños, aunque me gusta aún más comprar regalos para otras personas. Lo que no aguanto son las bodas.

Javier

Siempre que mi familia y yo nos reunimos, hablamos durante horas después de comer. Esta costumbre se llama sobremesa y creo que es genial.

Blanca

Match the correct person with each of the following questions.

Write **M** for Miguel, **A** for Andrés, **J** for Javier or **B** for Blanca.

1.1   Who does not like weddings?

1.2   Who likes chatting with family after lunch?

1.3   Who likes receiving presents?

1.4   Who spends Christmas Eve with their family?

1.5   Who likes buying presents?

1.6   Who enjoyed a family wedding?

1.1 J   1.2 B   1.3 J   1.4 A   1.5 J   1.6 M

Organising your writing

When putting together a piece of writing, it is a good idea to include time markers to organise your ideas.

You could organise paragraphs using words like **primero** *first*, **segundo** *second*, **tercero** *third*, **al final** *in the end*, **luego / entonces** *then*.

You could also order events by saying that something happened before something else (**antes de** + infinitive) or after (**después de** + infinitive).

2. Read this Spanish text. Add time markers and expressions from the box on the previous page to increase its complexity and to make it sound more natural. Make any other changes that you think may improve the quality of the text.

> Todos los años, celebro mi cumpleaños con mis amigos y con mi familia.
>
> Me levanto y tomo un desayuno inglés con mi familia.
>
> Abro mis regalos en el salón con mis padres y mis hermanos.
>
> Me visto y voy con mi familia a mi restaurante favorito.
>
> Por la tarde me gusta ver a mis amigos.
>
> Vamos al parque y vamos al cine.
>
> Vuelvo a casa cansado pero muy contento.

Here's an example of the reworded text. All changes are in red.

Todos los años, me apasiona celebrar mi cumpleaños tanto con mis amigos como con mi familia.

Primero, me levanto un poco tarde y tomamos juntos un desayuno inglés porque es mi desayuno favorito. Luego, vamos todos al salón y abro mis regalos con mi familia. ¡Es tan emocionante!

Después de vestirme, mi familia y yo vamos a mi restaurante favorito. ¡La comida es deliciosa!

Por la tarde, me gusta ver a mis amigos. Antes de ir al cine, nos gusta ir al parque.

Al final, vuelvo a casa cansado pero muy contento.

Now write your own text – what do you like to do to celebrate your birthday?

Role play

3. **H** Plan what you are going to say in this role play, taking into account the number of details you will need. Then play the recording, pausing after each question or statement so you can give your response. (This is a Higher tier role play).

TRACK 44

  3.1 Say what you normally do in the mornings. (Give **two** details.)

? 3.2 Ask your friend a question about their daily routine.

  3.3 Say what festival you would like to take part in. (Give **one** opinion and **one** reason.)

  3.4 Give your opinion about receiving money for your birthday.

  3.5 Say why you like family celebrations. (Give **one** opinion and **one** reason.)

CELEBRATIONS IN THE PAST AND FUTURE

Useful vocabulary

La Nochebuena	*Christmas Eve*	La Navidad	*Christmas*
La Nochevieja	*New Year's Eve*	El Año Nuevo	*New Year (Day)*
Los Reyes Magos	*the Three Kings (Epiphany – 6th January)*	Un regalo	*a present*
Un desfile	*a parade*	La comida de Navidad	*Christmas lunch*
Las uvas	*grapes*	La buena suerte	*good luck*

1. Read the following email. Mateo describes his Christmas celebrations to a friend in the UK.

   Write down whether the sentences refer to something happening now (**N**), something that happened in the past (**P**) or something that will happen in the future (**F**).

   Hola, Thomas,

   ¿Qué tal? Te escribo desde la casa de mis abuelos, donde estamos pasando las vacaciones de Navidad. Antes pasaba las Navidades en casa, pero desde hace tres años, preferimos venir al norte de España. Está nevando y hace frío, por eso hemos decidido que el diciembre que viene, vamos a pasar las Navidades en un país con mejor tiempo.

   Hace un momento, salimos para dar un paseo por el pueblo antes de volver a casa y tomar la cena de Nochebuena. En España no hay regalos el día de Navidad, así que aún tendré que esperar unos días para recibir mis regalos.

   Volveremos a casa para Nochevieja. No me gustan las uvas, por eso nunca he comido las uvas de la suerte, pero este año he decidido que voy a probarlas por primera vez.

   1.1   Spending Christmas at his grandparents' house.
   1.2   Spending Christmas at home.
   1.3   Experiencing cold weather.
   1.4   Spending Christmas in another country.
   1.5   Going for a walk.
   1.6   Receiving presents.
   1.7   Eating grapes for New Year's Eve.

   1.1 N   1.2 P   1.3 N   1.4 F   1.5 P   1.6 F   1.7 F

Dictation

2. Listen to these **five** sentences and write them down in **Spanish**. You will hear them once in full, a second time in sections, and once again in full the third time through.

TRACK 45

2.1 El invierno pasado / pasé la Navidad / con mis primos. 2.2 Prefiero recibir / dinero para mi cumpleaños. 2.3 El Carnaval es / la fiesta que / preferiría visitar. 2.4 Anoche / me desperté temprano. 2.5 Me gusta merendar / un vaso de leche.

¿Qué hiciste en Nochevieja?   *What did you do for New Year's Eve?*

The last part of your speaking exam is the photo card. You will have to talk about two photos for about **one minute** for Foundation or **one and a half minutes** for Higher. After that, you will have an unprepared conversation on the theme of the card, for three to four minutes for Foundation, or four and a half to five and a half minutes for Higher. You will need to demonstrate a variety of language, vocabulary and tenses as well as extending your responses to as many questions as possible.

3. Translate the following questions into English.

Then prepare answers for each of them in Spanish.

3.1 ¿Qué haces normalmente por las mañanas?

3.2 ¿A qué hora meriendas normalmente?

3.3 ¿Cómo celebraste tu cumpleaños el año pasado?

3.4 ¿Qué haces con tu familia en las vacaciones de Navidad?

3.5 ¿Dónde pasarás las vacaciones de Navidad en el futuro?

3.6 Describe una celebración reciente con tu familia

3.7 ¿Has visitado una fiesta en España?

3.8 ¿Cuáles son tus planes para tu próximo cumpleaños?

3.9 ¿Qué fiesta en España o Latinoamérica te gustaría visitar?

3.10 ¿Qué regalos te gustaría recibir en tu próximo cumpleaños?

3.1 What do you normally do in the mornings?   3.2 What time do you normally have a snack? 3.3 How did you celebrate your birthday last year?   3.4 What do you do with your family during the Christmas holidays?   3.5 Where will you spend your Christmas holidays in the future? 3.6 Describe a recent celebration with your family.   3.7 Have you visited a festival in Spain? 3.8 What are your plans for your next birthday?   3.9 Which festival in Spain or Latin America would you like to visit?   3.10 What presents would you like to receive at your next birthday?

Practise your responses to Q3 out loud – you could even record yourself and listen back to the recording. Look at the timings in the question box above to work out how long you will need to speak for (this time includes the questions as well as your answers).

CUSTOMS, FESTIVALS AND CELEBRATIONS

Ponerlo todo junto — *Putting it all together*

1. **F** Choose the correct option for the gap.
   This type of exercise appears in the Foundation writing exam only, with five sentences.

   1.1 Me encantaron los fuegos artificiales _____ en la fiesta local.
   bonito   bonita   bonitos

   1.2 Antes de _____ a la boda de mi tío, tengo que llamar a mi padre.
   ir   voy   voy a ir

   1.3 A mi hermano le gusta _____ por la mañana.
   se duchó   ducharse   se ducha

   1.4 El año que viene, _____ visitar la Tomatina.
   podré   podía   pude

   1.1 bonitos   1.2 ir   1.3 ducharse   1.4 podré

Photo card

2. Look at the two photos and make notes about what you can say about them. Then set a timer and talk about the content of the photos.

   Foundation **F** students have **one minute** to talk and Higher **H** students have a **minute and a half**. Then listen to the recording to hear an example of what could be said.

   TRACK 46

Photo 1

Photo 2

3. Translate the following into Spanish.

   3.1 In the mornings, I get up at 7.30.

   3.2 Last year, I went to a restaurant to celebrate my birthday.

   3.3 I would like to go to the festival because it would be interesting.

   3.4 **H** I have just come back from my auntie's wedding.

   3.5 **H** After having a shower, I will be able to watch TV.

   3.1 *Por la(s) mañana(s), me levanto a las siete y media.*

   3.2 *El año pasado, fui a un restaurante para celebrar mi cumpleaños.*

   3.3 *Me gustaría ir a la fiesta porque sería interesante.*

   3.4 *Acabo de volver de la boda de mi tía.*

   3.5 *Después de ducharme, podré / voy a poder ver la tele.*

4. **H** This student has written 75 words about a past visit to a festival in answer to the second bullet point of this Higher writing task. The full task would require **150 words**.

   Mention:
   - how you prefer to celebrate family events
   - a recent visit to a Spanish or Latin American festival.

   Hace dos años, mi familia y yo fuimos al Festival del Tango en Argentina, y lo pasé increíble. Había muchos espectáculos de baile y me encantó escuchar la música tan diferente. Un día, participamos en una clase de tango – era súper difícil, y después de bailar varias horas, estaba muy cansada. En el futuro cuando sea mayor, me gustaría ir a otras fiestas diferentes. Me parece que son muy importantes para la cultura del país.

   ! Note the variety of different tenses – the bullet point requires an answer in the past, and both the imperfect and preterite have been used to fulfil this. After that, there is a subjunctive, a conditional and a present tense.

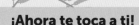

¡Ahora te toca a ti! *Your turn!*

5. You are emailing a friend about festivals and celebrations.

   Write approximately **150 words** in **Spanish**. You must write something about both bullet points.

   Mention:
   - how you prefer to celebrate family events
   - a recent visit to a Spanish festival.

CELEBRITY CULTURE

Mi celebridad favorita   *My favourite celebrity*

Useful vocabulary

casado/a	*married*	soltero/a	*single*
conocido/a	*well known*	latino/a	*Latin*
rico/a	*rich*	la riqueza	*wealth*
el actor	*actor*	la actriz	*actress*
la actuación	*performance*	la banda	*music band*
la canción	*song*	los seguidores	*followers*
la estrella	*star*	la industria	*industry*

1. Read these two texts about a famous actor and a famous singer.

Jorge Esteve es un actor español muy conocido. Está casado con una actriz española, Inés Gracia. Ha ganado muchos premios durante su carrera, incluyendo un Óscar. No solo ha trabajado en España, también es famoso por sus papeles en películas en Hollywood, donde ha interpretado a muchos villanos. No tiene presencia en las redes sociales.

Maribel es una cantante que tiene 17 millones de seguidores. Aunque nació en España y su padre es español, vive en México, donde es muy famosa. Es cantante, actriz y empresaria, y genera mucho interés en las redes sociales. Canta en inglés además de español. Tiene muchos premios musicales. Está soltera en este momento.

Do these sentences apply to Jorge (**J**), Maribel (**M**) or both (**J + M**)?
1.1 Has many followers on social media.
1.2 Can speak more than one language.
1.3 Has more than one job.
1.4 Is married.
1.5 Has won awards.
1.6 Lives in Spain.
1.7 Is Spanish.

1.1 M   1.2 M   1.3 M   1.4 J   1.5 J + M   1.6 J   1.7 J + M

2. Listen to an extract of an interview with César Vallejo, a Chilean YouTuber, and answer the questions in **English**.

2.1 How did César's interest in media start?

2.2 Why did he decide to start on YouTube?

2.3 What advantage of being a YouTuber does César mention?

2.4 What are the disadvantages?

2.5 What topics does César talk about on his channel?

2.1 He used to help at the school radio and then started to work for Chile's national radio.

2.2 He can talk about more varied topics / he doesn't have to follow company rules.

2.3 You can be your own boss.

2.4 His hours are not strict / he often works weekends and evenings.

2.5 Current news and celebrity interviews.

In listening exercises, sometimes you are going to need more than one piece of information to get a mark. If you hear two answers to the question, and they do not contradict each other, write both.

Using connectors

When writing and speaking in Spanish, it is important to use a wide variety of connectors to extend and add complexity to your sentences.

Some of the most useful ones are:

ya no *no longer*	porque *because*	ya que *since*	y *and*	aunque *although*

mientras *meanwhile / whilst*	pero *but*	por eso *that's why*	sin embargo *however*

3. Write some sentences about your favourite celebrities, making sure that each sentence includes at least one of the connectors above. You could talk about what they do, what they look like, where they can be followed or why you like them. Look at the examples below.

Me encanta seguir a Salma Hayek **porque** me interesan sus películas.

Algunas celebridades ayudan a otras personas, **por eso** las sigo.

Ya no uso Instagram para leer sobre personas famosas **ya que** me parece aburrido.

PROFILE OF A CELEBRITY

¿A quién sigues?   *Who do you follow?*

1. Read this interview with Rafaela, a Colombian footballer.

Rafaela, ¿siempre te ha gustado el fútbol?

No, cuando era pequeña en la escuela las niñas no podían jugar al fútbol, así que yo no empecé a jugar hasta los doce años. Jugaba con mi hermano y sus amigos, y siempre les ganaba.

¿Piensas que tienes una gran influencia por tu fama en tu país?

Creo que las personas famosas tenemos mucha más influencia que antes, por la importancia de los medios de comunicación. Por ejemplo, acabo de hacer una entrevista que puedes ver en YouTube, y espero que algunas chicas la escucharán y querrán jugar al fútbol.

¿Te interesa el lujo que disfrutan muchos futbolistas?

No me importa tener muchas cosas porque no soy muy materialista. Lo que quiero es usar mi fama para que algún día todos los géneros tengan igualdad de oportunidades.

Find in the text ...

1.1 four verbs in the imperfect tense.

1.2 one verb in the preterite tense.

1.3 seven verbs in the present tense.

1.4 two verbs in the future tense.

1.5 one verb in the present subjunctive.

1.6 one expression that means 'I have just done'.

1.1   era, podían, jugaba, ganaba

1.2   empecé

1.3   creo, tenemos, acabo, puedes, espero, importa, soy, quiero

1.4   escucharán, querrán

1.5   tengan

1.6   acabo de hacer

When you have a text with different tenses, do not assume that each paragraph will include just one time frame. To make it more challenging, the likelihood is that tenses will be mixed up. Also look out for expressions like **acabo de**, which actually expresses a past time frame, and **tengo la intención de**, which refers to the future.

2. Read aloud this passage and then listen to the recording to check your pronunciation.

TRACK 48

> Mi celebridad favorita es una actriz mexicana que se llama Aurora. Es importante que los actores latinos sean tratados con igualdad. No me interesan los famosos en Internet porque son una pérdida de tiempo.

3. **⒡** Choose the correct option for the gap.
   This type of exercise appears in the Foundation writing exam only.

   3.1 Voy a _____ un vídeo en YouTube.
   ver   veo   vi

   3.2 Esteban Aguirre es una _____ estrella en México.
   grande   grandes   gran

   3.3 El sábado pasado, yo _____ con mi hermano a un concierto.
   fue   fui   fueron

   3.4 Algún día, yo _____ ser una persona famosa.
   quise   querría   quería

4. You are writing an article about celebrity culture.

   Write approximately **90 words** in **Spanish**.

   You must write something about each bullet point. (See below for an example answer to the second bullet point.)

   Mention:

   - the best thing about your favourite celebrity
   - how you followed a celebrity last weekend
   - what you would do in the future in order to be famous.

   3.1 ver   3.2 gran   3.3 fui   3.4 querría

   4.
   > *El fin de semana pasado, usé mi móvil para ver vídeos en YouTube de mi cantante favorito. Vi una entrevista que hizo el mes pasado, y también escuché algunas canciones. Es una buena manera de pasar el tiempo libre.*
   >
   > **39 words**

REALITY TV

Los programas de telerrealidad — Reality TV programmes

Useful vocabulary

el comportamiento	*behaviour*	la pareja	*couple / partner*
el éxito	*success*	tener éxito	*to be successful*
la prensa	*press*	la voz	*voice*
el anuncio	*advert / announcement*	engañar	*to cheat*
la carrera	*career / race*	la entrevista	*interview*
mundial	*worldwide*	apropiado/a	*appropriate*

Modal verbs

These verbs are followed by an infinitive in Spanish. Many of them are irregular in some tenses and/or persons. The table below shows some common modal verbs in the **yo** form.

Infinitive	English	Present	Preterite	Future
deber	*must*	debo	debí	deberé
poder	*to be able to*	puedo	pude	podré
querer	*to want*	quiero	quise	querré
tener que	*to have to*	tengo que	tuve que	tendré que
saber	*to know*	sé	supe	sabré

Other uses:

quisiera *I would like*

podría *I would be able to / I could*

debería *I should*

se puede *you / one can*

se debe *you / one must*

hay que *one has to / you have to*

---

1. Translate the following sentences into **English**.

   1.1 Lo que más me molesta de Internet es que no se pueden evitar los anuncios.

   1.2 Voy a comprar un móvil nuevo y querré usarlo todo el tiempo.

   1.3 Ayer, tuve que ver una entrevista en la televisión con mis padres.

   1.4 Debería dejar de mirar mi móvil y hacer mis deberes.

   1.5 En X, hay que escribir mensajes muy cortos.

1.1 What annoys me (the) most about the Internet is that you cannot avoid adverts.
1.2 I am going to buy a new mobile and I will want to use it all the time.   1.3 Yesterday, I had to watch an interview on the TV with my parents.   1.4 I should stop looking at my mobile and do my homework.   1.5 On X, you have to write very short messages.

2. Read these messages found on social media about different reality TV programmes.

> No me gusta nada **Gran Hermano** – me pone nervioso mirar a personas *encerradas en una casa. El comportamiento puede ser terrible.

> **Operación Triunfo** ha ayudado a algunos cantantes con mucho talento a conseguir éxito mundial. Sus voces son maravillosas. Sin embargo, el programa es demasiado largo.

> Gracias a **MasterChef Celebrity** he aprendido un poco más sobre la personalidad de una de mis celebridades favoritas que participó el año pasado.

> Lo más interesante de **Supervivientes** es ver cómo los participantes buscan soluciones a problemas. Es muy emocionante.

Which programme ...

2.1 has helped some people become successful?
2.2 has revealed details about a celebrity's character?
2.3 is uncomfortable to watch?
2.4 allows you to enjoy singers' voices?
2.5 is exciting to watch?
2.6 is too long?

> ***encerrado** = *locked up*

2.1 Operación Triunfo   2.2 MasterChef Celebrity   2.3 Gran Hermano   2.4 Operación Triunfo
2.5 Supervivientes   2.6 Operación Triunfo

Dictation

3. You will hear four sentences, repeated three times. Write them down in **Spanish**.
(Note that on the Higher ❶ paper there are five sentences).

3.1 El jamón / en el bocadillo / está riquísimo.
3.2 Hay / unas cuantas gotas / en la mesa.
3.3 Me apasiona / tocar / la guitarra.
3.4 Los jardines / son relajantes / pero demasiado largos.

➕ Remember

Remember that **j** and **g** can have the same sound. **j** + **a/o/u** and **g** + **e/i** are similar to the 'ch' in the Scottish word 'loch'.

For a 'g' sound like in the word 'garden', you will need **g** + **a/o/u** or **gu** + **e/i**.

CELEBRITIES AS ROLE MODELS

Los ejemplos a seguir   *Role models*

Useful vocabulary

ayuda a las personas que lo necesitan	*helps people who need it*	representa organizaciones benéficas	*represents charities*
ayuda a otras personas	*helps other people*	da dinero	*donates money*
es un buen / mal ejemplo a seguir	*is a good / bad role model*	se comporta bien / mal	*behaves well / badly*
no sigue la ley	*does not follow the law*	no paga impuestos	*does not pay taxes*
fuma	*smokes*	demasiado alcohol	*too much alcohol*
toma drogas	*takes drugs*	gasta demasiado en las cosas de lujo	*spends too much on luxury items*

Ⓗ Using different persons of the verb in your writing

When putting together a piece of writing, try to include verbs in the third person singular and plural, not just in the first person. This will add variety and complexity to your writing.

The table below shows some of the verbs that have a different stem in the first and third persons. Some have additional changes in spelling.

	Present		Preterite	
	'I' form	'he/she' form 'they' form	'I' form	'he/she' form 'they' form
seguir	sigo	sigue siguen	seguí	siguió siguieron
poner	pongo	pone ponen	puse	puso pusieron
tener	tengo	tiene tienen	tuve	tuvo tuvieron
hacer	hago	hace hacen	hice	hizo hicieron
ir	voy	va van	fui	fue fueron
dirigir	dirijo	dirige dirigen	dirigí	dirigió dirigieron
gustar	me gusta(n)	le gusta(n) les gusta(n)	me gustó / gustaron	le/les gustó gustó/gustaron

1. Translate the following sentences into **Spanish**. Use the information on the previous page to help you.

   1.1 I followed the singer on social media to see how he helps other people.

   1.2 Some celebrities have too much money and spend too much on luxury items.

   1.3 Yesterday, I put on the television to watch a concert.

   1.4 My parents like celebrities who give money to people that need it.

   1.5 The footballer made a mistake when he did not pay his taxes.

   1.1 *Seguí al cantante en las redes sociales para ver cómo ayuda a otras personas.*

   1.2 *Algunas celebridades tienen demasiado dinero y gastan demasiado en las cosas de lujo.*

   1.3 *Ayer, puse la televisión para ver un concierto.*

   1.4 *A mis padres les gustan las celebridades que dan dinero a las personas que lo necesitan.*

   1.5 *El futbolista hizo un error cuando no pagó sus impuestos.*

Role play

TRACK 50

2. **F** **H** Plan what you are going to say in this role play, taking into account the number of details you will need. Then play the recording, pausing after each question or statement so you can give your response.

   2.1 Say why you like your favourite celebrity. (Give **two** details.)

   ? 2.2 Ask your friend a question about fame.

   2.3 Say how you normally follow celebrities.

   2.4 Give your opinion about social media.

   2.5 Say what reality TV programmes you prefer.

3. Write about **75 words** describing one celebrity you like and why, and one that you don't like and why. You could write about what they do that is positive and negative.

The writing exercise above requires you to start your answer in the present tense. However, you need to make sure that you show enough complexity by including verbs in other tenses and persons, as well as complex vocabulary and structure.

PROS AND CONS OF FAME

Ventajas y desventajas   *Advantages and disadvantages*

Useful vocabulary

Ventajas *Advantages*	
Puedes tener mucha influencia.	*You can have a lot of influence.*
Ganas mucho dinero.	*You earn a lot of money.*
Puedes comprar casas y coches caros.	*You can buy expensive houses and cars.*
Te da la oportunidad de ser famoso/a.	*It gives you the opportunity to be famous.*
Puedes conocer a personas interesantes.	*You can meet interesting people.*
Recibes regalos de muchas personas y empresas.	*You receive presents from many people and companies.*

Desventajas *Disadvantages*	
No tienes vida privada.	*You don't have a private life.*
Las personas quieren conocerte solo por tu fama.	*People want to meet you just because of your fame.*
La fama no dura para siempre.	*Fame does not last forever.*
Todo el mundo expresa su opinión sobre tu comportamiento.	*Everyone gives / expresses their opinion about your behaviour.*
Tienes que ser guapo/a y delgado/a.	*You have to be good-looking and slim.*

1. Listen to these four people expressing their opinions about fame. Do they express a positive (**P**), negative (**N**) or positive and negative (**P + N**) opinion?

    TRACK 51

    1.1 Alba: _____   1.3 Eduardo: _____

    1.2 Toñi: _____   1.4 Juan: _____

2. Listen again.

    Write in English what reasons they give for their opinions. Write as much detail as possible.

    2.1 Alba: _____

    2.2 Toñi: _____

    2.3 Eduardo: _____

    2.4 Juan: _____

    1.1 N   1.2 P   1.3 P + N   1.4 P + N

    2.1 You may earn a lot of money, but it's not worth it because everyone watches everything you do.

    2.2 Fame doesn't last forever, but while it lasts, it can make your life more interesting.

    2.3 You can buy very expensive things, but you don't have a private life.

    2.4 You meet people who are only interested in your fame, but you receive a lot of free things.

Indefinite adjectives

Cada *each* does not change for number or gender.

Mismo *same*, **otro** *other / another* and **todo** *all / every* change for gender and number.

Algún *some* and **ningún** *no / neither / not ... any* go in front of a masculine noun.

When used in front of a feminine noun, they are **alguna** and **ninguna**, and their plural forms are **algunos / algunas**. The plural forms **ningunos** and **ningunas** are not used.

Ⓗ Alguno *some* and **ninguno** *none* are pronouns. This means that they aren't used with a noun like the adjectives above; they are used instead of a noun.

3. Read and match up the **Spanish** and the **English**.

   Then fill in the gaps with one of the words from the box above, changing the endings if needed.

3.1	¿Prefieres a Esteban o a Pablo? _____.	**A**	Do you prefer Esteban or Pablo? Neither.
3.2	_____ persona debería criticar a los demás.	**B**	I don't have any friends.
3.3	_____ día, seré famoso.	**C**	I don't like all celebrities' behaviour.
3.4	No me gustan _____ los comportamientos de las celebridades.	**D**	I follow some celebrities on my mobile.
3.5	No tengo _____ amigo.	**E**	I have the same T-shirt as you.
3.6	Sigo a _____ celebridades en mi móvil.	**F**	I watch videos on my tablet each day.
3.7	Tengo la _____ camiseta que tú.	**G**	Nobody should criticise other people.
3.8	Veo videos en mi tableta _____ día.	**H**	Someday, I will be famous.

3.1 A – ninguno   3.2 G – ninguna   3.3 H – algún   3.4 C – todos   3.5 B – ningún
3.6 D – algunas   3.7. E – misma   3.8 F – cada

4. Translate into **Spanish**.

   4.1 Someday, I will buy an expensive car.

   4.2 I don't have any songs on my mobile.

   4.3 I listen to music each day.

   4.4 Some people are unpleasant online.

4.1 Algún día, compraré un coche caro.   4.2 No tengo ninguna canción en mi móvil.
4.3 Escucho música cada día.   4.4 Algunas personas son antipáticas en línea.

CELEBRITY CULTURE

Ponerlo todo junto   *Putting it all together*

1. ❶ Choose the correct option for the gap.
   This type of exercise appears in the Foundation writing exam only.

   1.1 Mis padres no _____ usar el móvil para mandar mensajes en las redes sociales.
   pueden   puede   poden

   1.2 Hay _____ celebridades que dan mal ejemplo a los jóvenes.
   algún   algunos   algunas

   1.3 Mi hermano _____ muchas apps en su teléfono.
   tiene que   tiene   tengo

   1.4 Quiero _____ a Shakira en la televisión.
   vi   veo   ver

   1.1 pueden   1.2 algunas   1.3 tiene   1.4 ver

2. Listen to a conversation between two Spanish teenagers, Alejandra and Nicolás.
   Read the sentences below. Who expresses these opinions?

   TRACK 52

   Alejandra (**A**), Nicolás (**N**) or both (**A + N**)?

   2.1 There are more disadvantages than advantages to fame.

   2.2 One positive aspect is that you receive many presents.

   2.3 People criticise celebrities' appearance.

   2.4 People criticise celebrities' clothes.

   2.5 Celebrities don't care about people's needs.

   2.6 Celebrities have lives full of luxury.

   2.7 Celebrities deserve to have luxuries.

   2.1 A   2.2 A + N   2.3 A + N   2.4 A   2.5 A   2.6 A + N   2.7 N

3. ❷ This student has written **75 words** about a past visit to a festival in answer to the second
   bullet point of this Higher writing task. The full task would require **150 words**.

   Mention:
   - an advantage and a disadvantage of being a celebrity
   - if you would like to be famous in the future.

   Creo que odiaría ser famoso en el futuro. Primero, no me gustaría recibir críticas todo el tiempo sobre mi ropa, mi aspecto físico y mi personalidad. Creo que algunas celebridades tienen demasiada influencia en los jóvenes y para mí es una responsabilidad demasiado grande. Yo preferiría tener un trabajo en el que podría ayudar a otras personas. Algunas celebridades tienen un comportamiento terrible, creo que si eres famoso debes ser un buen ejemplo a seguir.

Photo card

4. Look at the two photos and prepare ideas on what to say about them. Remember to say something about both photos and to talk for one minute (**F**) or one and a half minutes (**H**). Then listen to the recording to hear an example of what could be said.

TRACK 53

Photo 1

Photo 2

5. You are emailing a friend about celebrities.

Write approximately **150 words** in **Spanish**.

You must write something about both bullet points.

Mention:

- an advantage and a disadvantage of being a celebrity
- if you would like to be famous in the future.

KEY VOCABULARY

Students are expected to know 1200 items of vocabulary for Foundation tier and a further 500 for Higher tier. This list has some of the key vocabulary for Theme 2, but there are many more words listed in the AQA specification and in an interactive spreadsheet on the AQA website.

famoso	famous
los medios de comunicación	media
la canción	song
la fiesta	party, festival
la moda	fashion
la música	music
la película	film
la telerrealidad	reality TV
seguir	to follow
el / la modelo	model
rico	rich
divertido	fun, enjoyable
al aire libre	in the open air, outdoors
Día de Muertos	Day of the Dead (Mexican celebration)
la boda	wedding
Navidad	Christmas
la tradición	tradition
las tapas	small dishes of food, bar snacks
bailar	to dance
el regalo	present, gift
celebrar	to celebrate
pasarlo bien / mal	to have a good / bad time
el centro comercial	shopping centre
la bici / bicicleta	bike / bicycle
la comida	food, meal, lunch
la piscina	swimming pool
los amigos / las amigas	friends
el cine	cinema
el perro	dog
dar un paseo	to go for a walk
tomar el sol	to sunbathe
el parque temático	theme park
jugar	to play (a game or sport)

EXAMINATION PRACTICE

Popular culture – Reading

These people have written their opinions about free time on their school's web page.

Ana
Aunque no me importan los deportes de equipo, lo que realmente no aguanto son los deportes individuales. Me aburren porque soy sociable. También voy al gimnasio a menudo para mantenerme en forma.

Miguel
Creo que la mejor manera de pasar un fin de semana con la familia es cocinar juntos. No entiendo a las personas que solo comen comida rápida. Los productos frescos son mejores para ti.

Paco
Para mí, montar a caballo es una actividad relajante. Me encanta estar al aire libre y en contacto con la naturaleza. Mi familia también lo practica, pero yo prefiero montar solo. Antes, iba al gimnasio todos los días, pero ya no.

Inés
Doy paseos con frecuencia para mantenerme sana y feliz. Sin embargo, me gustan mucho las hamburguesas y las patatas fritas, así que podría estar más saludable. Debería cambiar mi dieta.

Answer the following questions. Write **A** for Ana, **M** for Miguel, **P** for Paco or **I** for Inés.
Write the correct letter on each line.   [8 marks]

01 Who goes to the gym frequently? _____

02 Who prefers fresh food? _____

03 Who does not mind team sports? _____

04 Who likes to be outdoors? _____

05 Who does not have a healthy diet? _____

06 Who likes to spend time with family? _____

07 Who does not go to the gym anymore? _____

08 Who likes walking? _____

Translate these sentences into **English**.   [10 marks]

09 Estoy leyendo en mi dormitorio.

10 La semana pasada, hice natación en la piscina de mi pueblo.

11 Cuando era pequeño, iba al cine con mis padres.

12 Antes de ir a la fiesta, tengo que vestirme.

13 Ningún famoso quiere compartir toda su vida en las redes sociales.

Popular culture – Listening

Listen to these four people talking about celebrities. What are their opinions of them?
Write **P** for a positive opinion, **N** for a negative opinion and
P + N for a positive and negative opinion.

TRACK 54

[4 marks]

01 Alba: _____

02 Pedro: _____

03 Amaya: _____

04 Gabriel: _____

---

05 Listen to this footballer talking about his life.

Write **A** if only statement A is correct, **B** if only statement B is correct,
and **A + B** if both statements A and B are correct.

TRACK 55

[5 marks]

05.1 Marcelo plays... _____

    A for a Spanish team.

    B for an Argentinian team.

05.2 Marcelo... _____

    A likes the atmosphere in the team.

    B finds training challenging.

05.3 Marcelo thinks that... _____

    A some of his team mates do not make enough effort.

    B talent is not enough to make you successful.

05.4 Marcelo... _____

    A plans to play for 22 more years.

    B is 22 years old.

05.5 Marcelo's dream is... _____

    A to travel the world.

    B to play in an international competition.

Dictation

06 You will now hear five short sentences. (Note that, on the Foundation ❺ paper, there are
only four sentences.) Listen carefully and, using your knowledge of Spanish sounds, write
down in **Spanish** exactly what you hear for each sentence. You will hear each sentence
three times: the first time as a full sentence, the second time in short sections and the third
time again as a full sentence.

TRACK 56

Use your knowledge of Spanish sounds and grammar to make sure that what you have
written makes sense. Check carefully that your spelling is accurate.

[10 marks]

Popular culture – Speaking

Role play

H Plan what you are going to say in this role play, taking into account the number of details you will need. Remember you will need a verb in each response.

Then play the recording, pausing after each question or statement so you can give your response. (This is in the style of a Higher tier role play).

When you see this –**?**– you will have to ask a question.

TRACK 57

You are talking to your Colombian friend.   [10 marks]

    01 Say what you think about team sports. (Give **two** opinions.)

? 02 Ask your friend a question about watching sports on television.

    03 Say what the advantages are of watching a film at the cinema. (Give **one** advantage.)

    04 Say what you did with your friends last weekend. (Give **two** details.)

    05 Say if you play a musical instrument or not (Give **one** detail.)

Photo card

06 Look at the two photos and prepare ideas on what to say about them.
Remember to say something about both photos and to talk for one minute (Foundation **F**)
or one and a half minutes (Higher **H**).   [5 marks]

Photo 1

Photo 2

07 After you have talked about the card, listen to the recording.
Pause after you hear each question and try to answer them in as much detail as possible.
This part of the exam should last between three and four minutes for Foundation tier **F**,
and between four and a half and five and a half minutes for Higher tier **H**.

TRACK 58

[20 marks]

Popular culture – Writing

01 **F** You decide to send this photo on WhatsApp to a friend in Spain.

What is in this photo? Write **five** sentences in **Spanish**. Foundation only. [10 marks]

02 Translate the following sentences into **Spanish**. [10 marks]

(This is aimed at top **F** to **H** level).

2.1 I am cooking dinner for my parents.

2.2 I played piano in a concert last night.

2.3 After the festival, we could go to the beach.

2.4 I no longer watch documentaries on TV.

2.5 I think that celebrities should give a good example to young people.

03 You are writing to your Spanish friend about what you like to do in your free time.

Write approximately **90 words** in **Spanish**. You must write something about each bullet point.

(This is a **F** and **H** task.) [15 marks]

Mention:
- how you would like to celebrate your birthday next year
- if you prefer to go out with lots of friends or your best friend
- something a celebrity did that you did not like.

04 **H** You are writing an article for the school newsletter about how young people live.

Write approximately **150 words** in **Spanish**. You must write something about both bullet points.

(This is a Higher task.) [25 marks]

Mention:
- a weekend in the past when you had problems
- a description of a celebrity that gives a good example to young people today.

TOPICS FOR THEME 3
Communication and the world around us

Specification coverage

Topic 1   Travel and tourism, including places of interest

Topic 2   Media and technology

Topic 3   The environment and where people live

Information about the four papers for Foundation 🄵 and Higher 🄷 tiers:

Paper 1 – Listening

Written exam:
35 minutes 🄵, 45 minutes 🄷
40 marks 🄵, 50 marks 🄷
25% of GCSE

The recording is controlled by the invigilator with built-in repetitions and pauses.

Each exam includes 5 minutes' reading time at the start of the question paper before the listening material is played and 2 minutes at the end of the recording to check your work.

Section A – Listening comprehension questions in English, to be answered in English or non-verbally (🄵 32 marks, 🄷 40 marks).

Section B – Dictation where students transcribe 4 sentences (🄵 8 marks) or 5 sentences (🄷 10 marks).

Paper 2 – Speaking

Non-exam assessment (NEA):
7–9 minutes 🄵 or 10–12 minutes 🄷 +
15 minutes' supervised preparation time
50 marks, 25% of GCSE

Role play – 10 marks, 1-1.5 minutes. 🄵 🄷

Reading aloud passage and short conversation – 15 marks.
Recommended time 2-2.5 minutes 🄵 and 3-3.5 minutes 🄷.
Minimum 35 words 🄵 and minimum 50 words 🄷.

Photo card discussion (two photos) – 25 marks.
Photo card discussion time:
4-5 minutes 🄵 and 6-7 minutes 🄷.

Paper 3 – Reading

Written exam: 45 minutes 🄵, 1 hour 🄷
50 marks, 25% of GCSE

Section A – Reading comprehension questions in English, to be answered in English or non-verbally (40 marks).

Section B – Translation from Spanish into English, minimum of 35 words 🄵 or 50 words 🄷 (10 marks).

Paper 4 – Writing

Written exam: 1 hour 10 minutes 🄵,
1 hour 15 minutes 🄷
50 marks, 25% of GCSE

Set of three short writing tasks. 🄵 only. 25 marks.

Translation of sentences from English into Spanish, minimum 35 words 🄵, or 50 words 🄷 (10 marks).

Produce a piece of writing in response to three compulsory bullet points, approximately 90 words in total. Choose from two questions (15 marks). 🄵 🄷

Open-ended writing task.
Two compulsory bullet points, approximately 150 words in total. Choose from two questions. (25 marks). 🄷 only.

TRANSPORTATION

El transporte — *Transport*

La bicicleta

El autobús

El avión

El barco

El coche

El metro

El tren

Ir a pie

Important phrases

montar en bicicleta
to ride a bike

ir en barco
to go by boat

conducir un coche
to drive a car

salir
to leave, depart

llegar (a)
to arrive (in / at)

---

1. Listen to these four people (1.1–1.4) talking. Each one mentions two types of transport but which one does each person decide to use?

   TRACK 59

   Write the answer in **English**.

   1.1 Train
   1.2 Walk / on foot
   1.3 Boat
   1.4 Underground / metro

It is very important to listen to the whole recording for each question before you choose your answer.

When two or more options are given, you need to listen to the other clues to work out which options should be rejected.

2. Translate these sentences into **English**.

   2.1 ¿A qué hora sale el tren?
   2.2 A los niños les gusta montar en bicicleta.
   2.3 Tenemos que coger el autobús mañana.
   2.4 Fuimos a Santander en barco.
   2.5 El autobús llegó a las nueve, un poco tarde.

   2.1 *What time does the train leave?*
   2.2 *The children like riding (their) bikes.*
   2.3 *We have to catch the bus tomorrow.*
   2.4 *We went to Santander by boat.*
   2.5 *The bus arrived at nine, a little late.*

Comparing different forms of transport

In English, when we compare things, we use the comparative form of the adjective, for example, 'more comfortable', 'less expensive' or 'faster'.

To do this in Spanish, use **más** for *'more'*, **menos** for *'less'*, and **que** for *'than'*.

To say *'as … as'* (The train is as cheap as the bus), use **'tan … como'** around the adjective:
El tren es tan barato como el autobús.

Examples

El tren es **más caro que** el autobús.	*The train is **more expensive than** the bus.*
El avión es **más rápido que** el barco.	*The plane is **faster than** the boat.*
El autobús **es menos cómodo**.	*The bus is **less** comfortable.*

 Note the irregulars:
mejor – *better, best*   **peor** – *worse, worst*

---

3. Read Rosa's description of transport in her town and answer the questions.

En mi pueblo, la mayoría de personas viaja en coche porque es más práctico y conveniente. Los autobuses son más baratos que ir en tren, pero no son muy frecuentes. Sería genial tener un metro porque es la mejor manera de evitar el tráfico, pero solo hay metro en las ciudades más grandes. Muy poca gente va en bicicleta porque hay mucho tráfico y dicen que es menos peligroso ir a pie. Cuando vamos de vacaciones, normalmente vamos en avión porque es mucho más rápido. Ir en barco es muy lento y los billetes son tan caros como los billetes de avión.

3.1 Why do most people travel by car?
3.2 What is good about travel by bus?
3.3 What is the problem with the bus service?

3.4 Why does Rosa want an underground system?
3.5 Why would people rather walk than go by bike?
3.6 Why does Rosa criticise boat travel?

3.1 It's more practical and convenient.
3.2 Cheaper than the train.
3.3 Buses are not very frequent.

3.4 Best way of avoiding traffic.
3.5 Lots of traffic, so walking is less dangerous.
3.6 It's slow, tickets are as expensive as the plane.

---

4. Read aloud the following passage and then listen to the recording of it.

TRACK 60

Ayer, cogí el barco para ir a Ibiza. No fue un viaje largo y llegué a las once. Había mucha gente en el puerto porque es Semana Santa y muchas familias iban de vacaciones. La isla es muy popular en verano cuando los jóvenes van para escuchar música y para bailar.

! **Note**

Remember that **'j'** and **'g'** (when 'g' is followed by 'i' or 'e') are pronounced like **'ch'** in 'lo**ch**'.

HOLIDAYS

Las actividades de vacaciones	Holiday activities

Useful vocabulary

quedarse en la cama	to stay in bed	relajarse	to relax
descansar	to rest	leer	to read
tomar el sol	to sunbathe	nadar en el mar / la piscina	to swim in the sea / the pool
jugar al tenis	to play tennis	ir de excursión	to go on a trip
ir de compras	to go shopping	dar un paseo / paseos	to go for a walk / walks
hacer actividades	to do activities	salir con (mis) amigos	to go out with (my) friends

+ Remember

When you talk about what you usually do in the holidays, you need the present tense.

Regular verbs	Reflexive verbs	Irregular verbs
Regular verbs (**descansar, tomar, leer, nadar**) have an **-o** ending for the first person (I).	Reflexive verbs, as well as the **-o** verb ending, need '**me**' in front of the verb (**me quedo, me relajo**).	Irregulars: **dar → doy, ir → voy, jugar → juego, hacer → hago, salir → salgo, preferir → prefiero**

1. Put the verbs in brackets into the '**yo**' form of the present tense.

Durante las vacaciones de verano, (**1.1 hacer**) muchas actividades diferentes y (**1.2 salir**) con mis amigos y con mi familia. A veces, (**1.3 jugar**) al tenis con mi hermano o (**1.4 dar**) un paseo con mi perro. Cuando hace buen tiempo, (**1.5 nadar**) en la piscina y (**1.6 tomar**) el sol. Los días de lluvia, (**1.7 relajarse**) en casa y (**1.8 leer**) una novela. Algunos días, (**1.9 ir**) de compras o de excursión con la familia. Nunca (**1.10 quedarse**) en la cama porque hay muchas cosas que (**11. preferir**) hacer.

1.1 hago	1.2 salgo	1.3 juego	1.4 doy
1.5 nado	1.6 tomo	1.7 me relajo	1.8 leo
1.9 voy	1.10 me quedo	1.11 prefiero	

Role play

TRACK 61

2. **F** **H** Prepare your responses and then listen to the recording, pausing after each question to give your answer. Remember to include a verb in each response.

- Say what you do in good weather during the holidays. (Give **one** detail.)
- Say what you do when it rains. (Give **one** detail.)
- Say what activities you do with family. (Give **two** details.)
- Ask your friend a question about their holiday activities.
- Say what you think about the activities you do with friends. (Give **one** detail.)

Talking about activities you are going to do in the future

To express the future, you can use either the immediate future or the future tense.

When you are talking about future holiday plans, you will mostly need these parts of the verbs:

Voy a + infinitive (*I am going to ...*)

Vamos a + infinitive (*We are going to ...*)

To use the future tense, take the infinitive (**-ar**, **-er**, **-ir**) and add **é** if you are talking about yourself, or **-emos** if you are talking about yourself and others.

For example:
iré – *I will go*, **nadaré** – *I will swim*, **viajaremos** – *we will travel*, **jugaremos** – *we will play*.

+ Remember

Remember that these verbs have slightly different stems in the future tense instead of the infinitive.

Foundation	tener – **tendr...**, hacer – **har...**, poder – **podr...**, poner – **pondr...**, **habrá** (*there will be*)
Higher	the above and: salir – **saldr...**, saber – **sabr...**, querer – **querr...**, venir – **vendr...**, decir – **dir...**

3. Read what Leo has written about his plans for the next summer holidays. The future tenses are in blue.

Este verano, vamos a pasar dos semanas en un camping cerca de la costa. Vamos a viajar en coche porque tendremos mucho equipo. Voy a nadar en el mar todos los días y jugaré al fútbol en la playa con mi hermano. Habrá otros jóvenes en el camping y espero hacer nuevos amigos. Saldremos juntos a las tiendas y daremos paseos en el campo. Quiero tomar el sol y relajarme. ¡Será genial!

Notice the use of **espero** + infinitive (*I hope to ...*) and **quiero** + infinitive (*I want to ...*). These are also considered to be an expression of a future time frame. These verbs also enable you to vary your language.

¡Ahora te toca a ti!   *Your turn!*

Write **60–70** words about your plans for the next school holidays. Use some of the ideas in Leo's account to help you.

DESCRIBING HOLIDAYS

Diferentes tipos de vacaciones   *Different holiday types*

How to say what you prefer

(Yo) prefiero ...	*I prefer ...*
Me gusta(n) más ...	*I like ... best.*
Para mí, lo ideal es / son ...	*For me, the ideal is / are ...*
Me encanta(n) ...	*I love ...*

 Always try to give reasons for your preferences and opinions.

 hacer camping *to go camping*

Different holiday types

las vacaciones ... *holidays*

... de sol y playa *sun and beach*	**... culturales** *cultural*	**... activas** *active*
... de invierno *winter*	**... en el campo** *in the country*	**... en el extranjero** *abroad*

---

1. Match each preference to the correct reason. (There is more than one possible answer.)

1.1	Yo prefiero las vacaciones de sol y playa ...		**A**	porque son tranquilas y relajantes.
1.2	Me gustan más las vacaciones culturales ...		**B**	porque me encanta nadar en el mar.
1.3	Para mí, lo ideal son las vacaciones activas ...		**C**	porque quiero probar nuevas actividades.
1.4	Prefiero hacer camping ...		**D**	porque me interesan el arte y la historia.
1.5	Me gustan más las vacaciones en el campo ...		**E**	porque me gusta cocinar al aire libre.

Possible answers include: 1.1 B   1.2 D   1.3 C   1.4 E   1.5 A

2. Think about two different types of holidays you like, then listen to the question and give your response. Use **también** (*also*) to link your comments about the two holiday types.

  TRACK 62

Talking about a holiday that went wrong

Useful phrases

Llegamos tarde.	*We arrived late.*	Perdieron nuestras maletas.	*They lost our cases.*
... no funcionaba(n).	*... did not work.*	Había un problema con el / la / los / las ...	*There was a problem with the ...*
Se rompió.	*It broke.*	Me quemé.	*I got sunburnt.*
Me rompí ...	*I broke ... (e.g. leg)*	Me puse enfermo/a.	*I got ill.*
No había sitio.	*There was no room.*	Estaba cerrado/a.	*It was shut.*
Perdí / perdimos ...	*I lost, missed / we lost, missed ...*	El viaje fue muy incómodo.	*The journey was very uncomfortable.*

3. This student has written **77 words** about a holiday disaster in answer to the second bullet point of this Higher writing task. The full task would require **150 words**.

   Mention:
   - how you prefer to spend your holidays
   - a recent holiday that went wrong.

   > Hace un año, fui a Menorca con mi familia y fue un desastre. Primero, llegamos tarde al aeropuerto y casi perdimos el avión. Cuando llegamos al hotel, había un problema con la habitación de mi madre – no funcionaba la luz. El primer día, me quemé cuando estaba tomando el sol, y el día después me puse enfermo. En la segunda semana, mi padre perdió su móvil y tuvo que ir a la policía. ¡No lo pasamos bien!

   ! Note the effective use of connectors: **y** and **cuando**.

   Note the time phrases that add variety: **hace un año**, **primero**, **el primer día**, **el día después**.

¡Ahora te toca a ti! — *Now it's your turn!*

4. You are emailing a friend about holidays.

   Write approximately **150 words** in **Spanish**.
   You must write something about both bullet points.

   Mention:
   - how you prefer to spend your holidays
   - a recent holiday that went wrong.

THE WEATHER

¿Qué tiempo hace? *What is the weather like?*

Useful vocabulary

Hace frío.	*It is cold.*	llover / llueve	*to rain / it rains*
Hace fresco.	*It is cool.*	Está lloviendo.	*It is raining.*
Hace viento.	*It is windy.*	la lluvia	*the rain*
Hace calor.	*It is hot.*	nevar / nieva	*to snow / it snows*
Hace sol.	*It is sunny.*	Está nevando.	*It is snowing.*
Hace buen / mal tiempo.	*It is good / bad weather.*	la nieve	*snow*
la temperatura	*temperature*	Hace / hay diez grados.	*It is ten degrees.*

1. Listen to the weather forecast. Which **two** types of weather are expected in **each** of these regions?

TRACK 63

   1.1 the centre: _____

   1.2 the north: _____

   1.3 the east: _____

   1.4 the south: _____

Answer in **English**.

1.1 snow, low temperatures   1.2 rain, cool   1.3 sunny, hot   1.4 cold, windy

2. You will often need to talk about events in the past. (See the notes on the preterite and imperfect on **pages 150-153**.) Read what these people say about how the weather affected their holiday plans.

What was the weather like and what did each one end up doing? Answer in **English**.

> *Queríamos ir a la playa, pero empezó a llover. Por eso, fuimos a visitar la catedral.*   **Ana**

> *Cancelaron la excursión en barco porque hacía viento. Decidimos dar un paseo.*   **Dani**

> *Íbamos a tomar el sol, pero hacía demasiado calor. Fuimos a la sala de juegos.*   **Alba**

> *Queríamos dar un paseo en bicicleta, pero estaba nevando y nos quedamos en casa.*   **Leo**

> *Fuimos a nadar en el mar, pero hacía mucho frío y decidimos ir de compras.*   **Martina**

Ana – started to rain, visited cathedral   Dani – windy, went for walk   Alba – too hot, went to games room   Leo – snowing, stayed at home   Martina – very cold, went shopping

3. Look back at the previous activity and adapt what the people say in order to translate these sentences.

   3.1 It started to snow and we decided to return to the hotel.

   3.2 We stayed at home because it was very cold.

   3.3 It was very windy so we did not go to the beach.

   3.4 It was very hot so we went to swim in the sea.

   3.5 We decided to go for a walk because the weather was good.

   3.1 Empezó a nevar y decidimos volver al hotel.

   3.2 Nos quedamos en casa porque hacía mucho frío.

   3.3 Hacía mucho viento así que no fuimos a la playa.

   3.4 Hacía mucho calor así que fuimos a nadar en el mar.

   3.5 Decidimos dar un paseo porque hacía buen tiempo.

> **Useful vocabulary**
>
> To say 'so', use **así que**.

Photo card

4. Look at the two photos and prepare ideas on what to say about them. Remember to say something about both photos and to talk for one minute (**F**) or one and a half minutes (**H**). Listen to the recording to hear a student talking about the photos.

TRACK 64

Photo 1

Photo 2

PLACES OF INTEREST

Los lugares de interés — *Places of interest*

Places you might visit on holiday

la plaza de toros	*the bullring*	la iglesia	*the church*
la isla	*the island*	la mezquita	*the mosque*
la(s) montaña(s)	*the mountain(s)*	el barrio	*the district*
el castillo	*the castle*	el jardín / los jardines	*the garden(s)*
el mercado	*the market*	el museo	*the museum*
el puerto	*the port*	el parque temático	*the theme park*

Adjectives to describe the places

cultural	*cultural*	famoso/a	*famous*
hermoso/a, bonito/a	*lovely / beautiful*	histórico/a	*historic*
tranquilo/a	*peaceful*	agradable	*pleasant*
antiguo/a, viejo/a	*old*	emocionante	*exciting*
educativo/a	*educational*	moderno/a	*modern*
nuevo/a	*new*	tradicional	*traditional*

1. Listen to these five people talking about the places they visit.
   Which **two** places does each person mention, and how do they describe them?

   1.1 beautiful / lovely mosque and peaceful gardens   1.2 educational museum and (very) old bullring   1.3 modern port and historic castle   1.4 exciting theme park and traditional market 1.5 cultural district and famous church

¡Ahora te toca a ti!   *Now your turn!*

4. Make up different sentences, following these examples and changing the place and adjective each time. Remember to make the adjectives agree. (See **pages 10-11** and **138-142** on adjectives).

   - Me gustó **el puerto** porque era muy **animado**.
   - Me gustaron **las montañas** porque eran muy **hermosas**.

Object pronouns

These are the main object pronouns you will need. They usually go before the verb in Spanish.

me	me	us	nos	to him / her	le
you (singular)	te	you (plural)	os	to them	les
him / it (m)	lo	them (m)	los		
her / it (f)	la	them (f)	las		

2. **❸** Complete the sentences with the correct object pronoun. Then translate the sentences into **English**.

2.1 Tengo una nueva camiseta; _____ compré en el mercado. *(it)*

2.2 Fuimos a la mezquita y el guía _____ explicó la historia del edificio. *(us)*

2.3 Si quieres ir al parque temático, _____ llevaremos allí mañana. *(you, singular)*

2.4 Los jardines son hermosos en primavera; _____ visitamos ayer. *(them)*

2.5 Visité el castillo esta mañana y _____ encontré muy interesante. *(it)*

2.6 Vi a mi hermano y _____ mostré las fotos del barrio histórico. *(to him)*

2.7 Las islas no están muy lejos; _____ vimos desde la montaña. *(them)*

2.1 *(la) I have a new T-shirt; I bought it at the market.*

2.2 *(nos) We went to the mosque and the guide explained the history of the building to us.*

2.3 *(te) If you want to go to the theme park, we will take you there tomorrow.*

2.4 *(los) The gardens are lovely in spring; we visited them yesterday.*

2.5 *(lo) I visited the castle this morning and I found it very interesting.*

2.6 *(le) I saw my brother and showed him the photos of the historic district.*

2.7 *(las) The islands are not very far; we saw them from the mountain.*

Dictation

3. **❸** You will hear five sentences, repeated three times. Write them down in **Spanish**. (Note that on the Foundation **❺** paper there are four sentences).

TRACK 66

3.1 *El ambiente / en el puerto / era animado.*

3.2 *Hay / una famosa historia / sobre la iglesia.*

3.3 *El edificio / es antiguo / y hermoso.*

3.4 *Los jardines / son tranquilos / y relajantes.*

3.5 *Pocos turistas / van a / la zona.*

+ Remember

Remember that the letter **h** is silent. There are three examples in this activity.

TRAVEL, TOURISM AND PLACES OF INTEREST

Ponerlo todo junto   *Putting it all together*

1. **H** This style of question is found on the reading paper at both tiers. It is called an 'inference' question because you have to infer or deduce what a word means from the context. These words are not from the defined vocabulary list.

What is a **chubasco**?

> Durante la semana hizo mucho sol, pero un día, cuando estábamos en el pueblo, hubo un **chubasco** y tuvimos que entrar en un bar para evitar la lluvia.

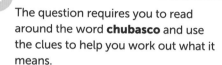

The question requires you to read around the word **chubasco** and use the clues to help you work out what it means.

If you just read **cuando estábamos en el pueblo**, then **chubasco** could mean any of the options given.

However, if you read further on, it says **tuvimos que entrar en un bar para evitar la lluvia** *we had to go into a bar to avoid the rain*. This extra information gives you the clue to the fact that **chubasco** means 'shower'.

A A parade
B A shower
C A traffic jam

2. **H** Now answer these questions in the same way.

2.1 What is a **gaita**?

> Durante nuestras vacaciones en el norte de España, fuimos a un espectáculo de baile tradicional. Algunos de los músicos tocaban un tipo de **gaita**, lo que me sorprendió porque no sabía que existía en España.

A A concert   **B** A dance   **C** A musical instrument

2.2 What is **horchata**?

> En Valencia, probé la famosa **horchata** que se sirve fría en un vaso alto y que se parece un poco a la leche. No me gustó mucho, pero a mi hermana sí.

A A drink   **B** A sandwich   **C** A soup

2.1 *C – It is a musical instrument. The text says that at a traditional dance show, the musicians were playing a type of 'gaita'. (It is similar to the Scottish bagpipes.)*

2.2 *A – It is a drink, served cold in a tall glass, and looks a little like milk.*

Reading aloud

3. Read aloud the following text in **Spanish**.

TRACK 67

> Por la mañana, queríamos ir al castillo, pero había muchos turistas allí. Por eso, dimos un paseo en los jardines botánicos y disfrutamos las vistas de la ciudad desde el puente. Visitamos el barrio antiguo, que era bastante tranquilo, y encontramos un restaurante genial. Hizo calor y sol todo el día.

Listen to the recording of the passage and check your pronunciation. Repeat any words you think you need to improve.

Now listen to the four recorded questions in Spanish that relate to travel, tourism and places of interest. Pause after each question to give your response. Try to answer all four questions as fully as you can.

Grammar gap fill

4. Complete the following sentences in **Spanish**. Write the correct word in the space.

4.1 Prefiero ir en tren porque es _____ cómodo.
   más   menos   poco

4.2 Mañana, _____ menos gente en la playa porque es lunes.
   hay   había   habrá

4.3 Vamos de vacaciones al extranjero porque siempre _____ aquí.
   lluvia   llover   llueve

4.4 El viaje en barco _____ horrible porque hizo mucho viento.
   es   fue   será

4.5 ¿Te gustan mis gafas de sol? _____ compré en el mercado.
   Me   Lo   Las

4.1 más   4.2 habrá   4.3 llueve   4.4 fue   4.5 Las

USING A SMARTPHONE

¿Cómo usas tu móvil?   *How do you use your mobile?*

Useful verbs

bajar	*to download*
buscar	*to look / search for*
compartir	*to share*
enviar	*to send*
grabar	*to record*
guardar	*to save / keep*
hacer / sacer fotos	*to take photos*
jugar (ue)	*to play*
llamar	*to call*
mandar	*to send*
mirar	*to look at*
subir	*to upload*

Nouns

la app	*app*
la cámara	*camera*
la información	*information*
el juego	*game*
la música	*music*
el mensaje	*(text) message*
el móvil	*mobile (phone)*
la página web	*web page*
la pantalla	*screen*
las redes sociales	*social networks*
el sitio web	*website*
en línea	*online*

1. Listen to these four young people taking part in a survey about how they use their mobile phone. Which **two** uses does each one mention?
TRACK 68

> *Martín: sends messages, looks up information online*
> *Isabel: takes photos, shares them on social networks*
> *José: downloads music, calls friends*
> *Rosa: plays games, looks at favourite websites*

Making the most of the infinitive (verbs ending in -ar, -er and -ir)

Notice how you can use the infinitive in many handy ways to answer questions. Using the vocabulary above in different ways, answer these questions.

¿Cómo usas tu móvil?
How do you use your mobile?

¿Por qué te gusta tu móvil?
Why do you like your mobile?

¿Es útil tener un móvil?
Is it useful to have a mobile?

Lo uso para ...
I use it to ...

Porque es muy útil para ...
Because it's very useful to ...

Sí, mucho, porque puedes ...
Yes, very, because you can ...

bajar música.
hacer fotos.
buscar información en línea.
jugar juegos.
subir y compartir fotos.
mandar mensajes.
llamar a los amigos.
mirar las redes sociales.

2. Your turn to answer the questions. Pause the recording after each one to give your response. Vary the vocabulary used so that you give different answers each time.
TRACK 69

Practising the perfect tense

If someone asks you **¿Cómo has usado tu móvil hoy?** they are using the perfect tense (*How have you used your mobile today?*). In English we would often use the simple past tense, where in Spanish the perfect tense would be used; for example: **He visto a Mario esta mañana**. *I saw Mario this morning*. This is how to form a sentence. (For more, see **page 152**.)

he		I have -ed	he bajado
has	**+ past participle**	You (singular) have -ed	has mandado
ha	(Remove **-ar** and add **-ado**,	He / she / it has -ed	ha respondido
hemos	remove **-er/-ir** and add **-ido**)	We have -ed	hemos entendido
habéis		You (plural) have -ed	habéis subido
han		They have -ed	han compartido

> **!** Most, but not all past participles in English end in **-ed**. Exceptions include "I have been", "they have eaten".

¿Cómo has usado tu móvil hoy?

He bajado música.

He llamado a mis padres.

He jugado juegos.

He buscado información en Internet.

He subido unas fotos a Instagram.

He mandado un mensaje a mi amigo.

He hecho* fotos.

> **!** Note the irregular form of **hacer** in the past participle – **hecho** *done / made*.

3. Translate the sentences into **Spanish** using the perfect tense.

   3.1 I have received your message.

   3.2 We have uploaded the information.

   3.3 Miguel has called his parents.

   3.4 Have you (singular) looked at the website?

   3.5 I have taken some photos today.

   3.6 We have recorded a message.

3.1 He recibido tu mensaje.
3.2 Hemos subido la información.
3.3 Miguel ha llamado a sus padres.
3.4 ¿Has mirado el sitio web?
3.5 He hecho unas / algunas fotos hoy.
3.6 Hemos grabado un mensaje.

THE INTERNET

El mundo de Internet · *The world of the Internet*

1. **H** Ángela has written an account of how her family uses the Internet. Read what she says.

> Yo no sé cómo vivíamos sin Internet en el pasado; en mi familia lo usamos para todo. Mi hermano es estudiante en la universidad y lo usa todo el tiempo para sus estudios. Dice que es ideal para hacer la investigación que necesita para sus proyectos. Mi madre lo usa para buscar información sobre los lugares que visitamos de vacaciones; hace reservas en hoteles, organiza vuelos y compra billetes de tren. Mi padre trabaja en casa y usa Internet para hacer videollamadas con sus compañeros de trabajo. También, le gusta mirar los comentarios de los clientes antes de reservar una mesa en un restaurante; luego consulta el menú en línea. Mi abuelo lo encuentra muy conveniente para hacer la compra del supermercado.

A	academic research	E	emailing family abroad	I	online shopping
B	booking flights	F	holiday research	J	playing online games
C	buying travel tickets	G	hotel booking	K	restaurant reviews
D	checking menus	H	lunch reservations	L	work video calls

How do these members of Ángela's family use the Internet? Write the correct letter or letters.

1.1 Brother: _____

1.2 Mother: _____

1.3 Father: _____

1.4 Grandfather: _____

1.1 A   1.2 F, G, B, C   1.3 L, K, H, D   1.4 I

Past, present, future?

A common question on the listening paper is to identify when an event takes place, whether in the past, now or in the future (P/N/F).

You need to listen out for the tenses of the verbs but also listen for time phrases:

2. Listen to these four people speaking and decide whether their Internet activity **TRACK 70** is in the past (**P**), now (**N**) or in the future (**F**).

2.1 N   2.2 P   2.3 F   2.4 P

Past

ayer *yesterday*, **anoche** *last night*, **hace dos días** *two days ago*, **la semana pasada** *last week*.

Now

ahora *now*, **hoy** *today*, **en este momento / de momento** *at the moment*.

Future

este sábado *this Saturday*, **mañana** *tomorrow*, **el domingo próximo / que viene** *next Sunday*

Sentence building

Read this sentence:

Mi madre usa Internet porque es ideal para mandar correos electrónicos.

My mum uses the Internet because it's ideal for sending emails.

Now use the ideas in this grid to say as many sentences as you can about how people in your family use the Internet.

| Mi ...
madre / padre
madrastra / padrastro
hermano / hermana
hermanastro / hermanastra
tío / tía
abuelo / abuela | usa
Internet
porque | es ideal para
es muy bueno para
es práctico para
es conveniente para
es muy útil para | ayudar con los estudios.
hacer las compras.
reservar vuelos / hoteles.
buscar información.
comprar billetes.
organizar las vacaciones.
hacer videollamadas.
trabajar en / desde casa.
mirar las redes sociales.
escuchar música. |

3. ⓗ Translate these sentences into **Spanish**.

   3.1 I use the Internet to look for information and to help with my studies.

   3.2 My sister worked from home last week.

   3.3 My father is going to organise the holiday and book the flights online.

   3.4 My grandfather uses the Internet a lot; it is very useful for making video calls.

   3.5 My brother bought his tickets on the website and booked the hotel.

   3.1 Uso Internet para buscar información y (para) ayudar con mis estudios.

   3.2 Mi hermana trabajó desde casa la semana pasada.

   3.3 Mi padre va a organizar las vacaciones y reservar los vuelos en línea / online.

   3.4 Mi abuelo usa Internet mucho; es muy útil para hacer videollamadas.

   3.5 Mi hermano compró sus billetes entradas en la página web y reservó el hotel.

> **!** Be careful – there are sentences here in the past, the present and the future.

SOCIAL MEDIA

Redes sociales   *Social networks*

Read these comments about social networks and answer the following questions.

"No hay mucha evidencia de que el uso de la tecnología esté asociado con problemas de salud mental." **Rafael**

"Si estás de mal humor en casa, vas a las redes sociales y te ríes y luego te sientes mejor." **Laura**

"En las redes sociales puedes conectarte con otras personas que comparten tus ideas e intereses." **Ana**

"Puedes mantenerte en contacto con familia y amigos que viven lejos." **David**

"Descubres nuevas formas de pensar, otros puntos de vista." **Sofía**

"Aprendes muchas cosas sobre el mundo por las iniciativas y campañas que ves, y puedes participar en actividades y eventos en la región donde vives." **Daniel**

1. **Ⓗ** Which person expresses each of the following opinion about social networks?

   1.1   They cheer you up when you're miserable.

   1.2   They're great for keeping in touch with people.

   1.3   You get to know people who like the same things as you.

   1.4   They make you more aware of what's happening locally and globally.

   1.5   There's not much proof that they have a bad effect on you.

   1.6   You learn about different views and opinions.

1.1 Laura   1.2 David   1.3 Ana   1.4 Daniel   1.5 Rafael   1.6 Sofía

2 **(H)** Listen to these four people talking about the negative side of social networks.

TRACK 71

Which view does each one express? Select the correct letter.

2.1 _____

    A They make you lose sleep.
    B They are a waste of time.
    C They are killing conversation.

2.2 _____

    A The photos are fake.
    B People are on their phone all the time.
    C It's all about people showing off.

2.3 _____

    A They make my life look dull.
    B I spend too much time on them.
    C I worry about security.

2.4 _____

    A Future employers might get the wrong impression.
    B Be careful about who can see your profile.
    C They make you want to change the way you look.

2.1 B   2.2 C   2.3 A   2.4 C

> Don't base your answer on recognising one word – it could be misleading.
>
> Ensure you listen to the whole recording and choose the answer that best fits.

Verbs with prepositions

You heard the verbs **tratar de** + infinitive (to try to) and **dejar de** + infinitive (to stop -ing) in the recording. As you can see, they take a following preposition (**de**) before the verb in the infinitive.

These verbs also take a following preposition:

acabar de *to have just*	**ayudar a** *to help to*	**acordarse de** *to remember to*	**aprender a** *to learn to*	**comenzar / empezar a** *to begin / start to*

enseñar a *to teach to*	**olvidarse de** *to forget to*	**preocuparse por** *to worry about*

3. **(H)** Translate these sentences into **English**.

   3.1 Las redes sociales me ayudan a mantenerme en contacto con mis primos en México.
   3.2 Me olvidé de subir las fotos de las vacaciones y mis amigos quieren verlas.
   3.3 Nos preocupamos por las imágenes falsas que los chicos y las chicas jóvenes ven en estos sitios web.

3.1 Social networks help me to keep in contact with my cousins in Mexico.
3.2 I forgot to upload the photos of the holiday and my friends want to see them.
3.3. We worry about (the) fake images that young boys and girls see on these websites.

TECHNOLOGY

Cuando la tecnología falla *When technology goes wrong*

Read what these people say about technology problems.

No pude llamarte, papá, porque me quedé sin batería.

Necesito consultar el mapa, pero aquí no hay señal.

Mira qué desastre. Se me cayó el móvil y la pantalla está rota.

No me lo creo. Me olvidé de guardar mi trabajo y lo he perdido todo.

Tengo una reunión de trabajo en línea, pero la cámara en el portátil no funciona.

La conexión a Internet es muy lenta, el ordenador va muy despacio.

1. Find the phrases.

  1.1 to save my work _____

  1.2 (it) doesn't work _____

  1.3 I dropped _____

  1.4 I ran out of battery _____

  1.5 (it) is going very slow _____

  1.6 there's no signal _____

  1.7 the screen is broken _____

  1.8 I've lost it all _____

1.1 guardar mi trabajo   1.2 no funciona   1.3 se me cayó   1.4 me quedé sin batería
1.5 va muy despacio   1.6 no hay señal   1.7 la pantalla está rota   1.8 lo he perdido todo

Role play

2. 🎧 Plan what you are going to say in this role play, taking into account the number of details you will need. Then play the recording, pausing after each question or statement so you can give your response.
   (This is in the style of a Higher tier role play).

TRACK 72

  2.1 Say how you use your mobile. (Give **two** details.)

  2.2 Say how someone in your family uses the Internet. (Give **two** details.)

  2.3 Give your opinion about social networks and a reason. (Give **one** opinion and **one** reason.)

  2.4 Give **one** example of a problem you have had with technology.

  ? 2.5 Ask your friend a question about technology.

Forming the imperfect continuous

Look at this sentence:

'I was calling my friend when **I ran out** of battery.'

The first verb is in the past continuous tense (was/were -ing) and the second verb is in the simple past tense (I ran out). You revised the Spanish equivalent of the simple past, the preterite, in 2.1 on **page 54**.

Take the imperfect tense of **estar**:

estaba *I was ...*

estabas *you (singular) were ...*

estaba *he / she / it was ...*

estábamos *we were ...*

estabais *you (plural) were ...*

estaban *they were ...*

add the present participle →

To form the present participle:

Verbs that end in **-ar**:
Remove the **-ar** and add **-ando**

Verbs that end in **-er** or **-ir**:
Remove the **-er/-ir** and add **-iendo**

Example

Estaba hablando. *I was talking.*
Estabas saliendo. *You (sing.) were leaving.*
Estaban compartiendo. *They were sharing.*

+ Remember

Because the verb ending of **estar** is the same for 'I' and 'he/she/it', you need to read the whole sentence to decide who is the subject of the verb (i.e. who is doing the action of the verb).

3. ❶ Translate these sentences into **English**.

   3.1 Estaba llamando a mi abuelo cuando me quedé sin batería.
   3.2 Martín estaba haciendo una videollamada cuando la cámara dejó de funcionar.
   3.3 Estaba haciendo mis deberes, pero me olvidé de guardar mi trabajo. ¡Qué desastre!
   3.4 Estábamos mirando el mapa, pero perdimos la señal y ahora no hay conexión.
   3.5 Se me cayó el móvil cuando estaba andando a la casa de mi amigo.

   3.1 I was calling my grandad when I ran out of battery.
   3.2 Martín was making a video call when the camera stopped working.
   3.3 I was doing my homework, but I forgot to save my work.
      What a disaster!
   3.4 We were looking at the map, but we lost the signal
      and now there's no connection.
   3.5 I dropped my mobile when I was walking to
      my friend's house.

THE IMPACT OF TECHNOLOGY

¿Qué impacto tiene la tecnología?   *What impact does technology have?*

1. **H** These people have posted their views on technology on a forum. Read them and decide whether each opinion is positive (**P**), negative (**N**) or a combination of both (**P + N**).

1.1   *Desde que compré un libro electrónico, creo que leo más que nunca. Es tan conveniente porque puedes cambiar el tamaño de las letras. También, cuando terminas una novela, puedes bajar la próxima en la serie enseguida.*

1.2   *La gran ventaja para mí es que ya no uso tanto papel, y la casa no está llena de mis documentos. Se puede guardar todo en el ordenador (y ¡se cortan menos árboles!).*

1.3   *Me preocupo a veces si puedo confiar en la información que encuentro. Algunas personas suben imágenes falsas o detalles incorrectos, y es fácil creerlo todo.*

1.4   *No cabe duda de que mis amigos se ponen muy perezosos cuando pueden escoger entre una actividad física y una hora más con sus videojuegos. Sin embargo, sin Internet sería más difícil organizar nuestros partidos de baloncesto.*

1.5   *Es genial poder buscar cualquier detalle en Internet sin tener que pasar horas tratando de acordarte de algo. Por otro lado, esto podría tener un impacto malo en la memoria — no tenemos que usarla tanto.*

1.1 P   1.2 P   1.3 N   1.4 P + N   1.5 P + N

+   **Remember**

When people give both positive and negative opinions, they are often connected by a word like **pero** *but*, **sin embargo** *however*, **aunque** *although*, **por otro lado** *on the other hand*. Listen out for these.

---

2. **H** Read comments 1.1–1.5 again and link each one to the correct summary.

A	Is it making my brain lazy?		**E**	It's tempting just to sit and play.
B	I just love my e-reader.		**F**	Can I trust anything I read?
C	It's good for the environment.		**G**	Parental controls are essential.
D	I set myself time limits.		**H**	Online bullying is widespread.

2.1 (1.1) B   2.2 (1.2) C   2.3 (1.3) F   2.4 (1.4) E   2.5 (1.5) A

Nouns with unexpected genders

Normally when a noun ends in **-o**, we expect it to be masculine, and if a noun ends in **-a**, we expect it to be feminine. This is not always the case, as you will see in the next activity.

3. Read this short passage and pick out eight nouns that don't behave as expected, in terms of the gender.

> La tecnología tiene muchas ventajas. Un día, puedes usarla para aprender un nuevo idioma y el día después, puedes ver un vídeo sobre cómo resolver un problema en tu casa. Por la tarde, puedes relajarte y ver un programa que has bajado online o compartir unas fotos con tus amigos en una red social. Claro que puede ser molesto cuando los sistemas fallan, y las redes sociales son un tema polémico*, pero con Internet tienes en la mano todos los conocimientos del mundo.

*polémico = *controversial*

el *día – day,* **el** *idioma – language,* **el** *problema – problem,* **el** *programa – programme,* **la** *foto – photo,* **el** *sistema – system,* **el** *tema – theme / topic,* **la** *mano – hand*

Photo card

4. Look at the two photos and prepare ideas on what to say about them. Remember to say something about both photos and to talk for one minute (**F**) or one and a half minutes (**H**). Listen to the recording to hear a student talking about the photos.

TRACK 73

Photo 1

Photo 2

MEDIA AND TECHNOLOGY

Ponerlo todo junto   *Putting it all together*

1. ⊕ Read this passage out loud and then check your pronunciation by listening to the recording of the passage. Then, answer the four recorded questions on technology that follow the passage.

TRACK 74

> Yo uso mi móvil para charlar con mis amigos y para llamar a mis padres si voy a llegar tarde. A veces, me gusta jugar juegos en el ordenador, pero mañana tengo que empezar un gran proyecto para el instituto y buscaré información en páginas web culturales y educativas.

Dictation

TRACK 75

2. ⊕ Listen to these five sentences and write them down in **Spanish**.
   You will hear them once in full, a second time in sections, and once again in full the third time through.

2.1   *Esta mañana, / organicé nuestras vacaciones / con mi ordenador.*

2.2   *He olvidado / la contraseña.*

2.3   *Tienes mi dirección / en el correo electrónico.*

2.4   *La imagen / en la foto / es falsa.*

2.5   *La pantalla / está rota.*

The 90-word writing task in the exam has three bullet points. One requires an answer in the present tense, one in the future tense and one in the past tense. It is very important to know the tenses well so you can say something in all three time frames.

Here is an example of a 90-word exam-style question that would be on both the Foundation and Higher papers. Look back through 'Media and technology' on **pages 106–115** and use the ideas to help you answer this question. Then look at the worked example underneath.

3. You are writing an article about technology.

Write approximately **90 words** in **Spanish**. You must write something about each bullet point.

Mention:
- why you think technology is useful
- a problem you had with technology in the past
- how you will use technology in the future.

Before having a go, take a look at the worked example below, then look back at the whole unit and write your own answer.

> The response is divided into three sections to clearly show that the three bullet points have been answered. Also note that the response is only just over the 90 words. It is quality not quantity that examiners are looking for.

Worked example

Gives a reason for the opinion

Uses the imperfect continuous tense, an example of complex language

Uses **para** (in order to) to give a list of three reasons and to create an extended sentence

Shows good knowledge of an irregular preterite in the first person singular

Demonstrates use of object pronouns and a regular preterite

Creo que la tecnología es esencial en el mundo moderno porque tiene muchos usos. Internet es útil para ayudar con los estudios, para buscar información y para mantenerte en contacto con amigos y familia.

La semana pasada, estaba escribiendo algo en el ordenador y cuando lo apagué, me olvidé de guardar mi trabajo. Lo perdí todo y tuve que empezar de nuevo.

Mañana, voy a usar mi móvil para organizar una excursión con mis amigos y voy a mirar el programa de películas en el cine. También, mandaré mis deberes a mi profesora por correo electrónico.   **96 words**

Shows good knowledge of verbs with prepositions and reflexive verbs, both examples of complex language

Shows good knowledge of the irregular verb **tener** in the preterite, and the construction **tener que** (to have to) + infinitive

Uses the immediate future tense

Uses the connector **también** (also), and the future tense

WHERE PEOPLE LIVE

Mi casa   *My house*

1. Read what Laura says about her new house.

> Antes, vivíamos en un piso en el centro de la ciudad, pero nuestra nueva casa está en las afueras. Tiene dos plantas y abajo están la cocina, el salón y el comedor. Subiendo la escalera, la primera puerta te lleva al baño y después están los tres dormitorios y el despacho de mis padres. Es un edificio moderno con ventanas grandes para dejar entrar la luz y un jardín detrás de la casa. No hay espacio para el coche así que lo aparcamos en la calle.

Find the following words:

floor / storey	kitchen	lounge
dining room	stairs	door
bathroom	bedroom	office
building	window	light
garden	space	street

floor / storey – la planta,   kitchen – la cocina,   lounge – el salón,   dining room – el comedor, stairs – la escalera,   door – la puerta,   bathroom – el baño,   bedroom – el dormitorio, office – el despacho,   building – el edificio,   window – la ventana,   light – la luz, garden – el jardín,   space – el espacio,   street – la calle

! Notice that Laura says **nuestra nueva casa está en las afueras**. Remember to always use the verb **estar** when you are saying or asking where someone or something is.

2. Use the vocabulary that you found in the text to describe this house.

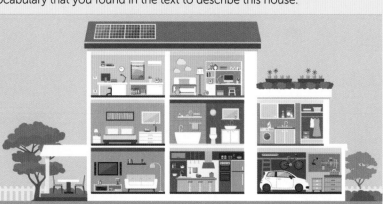

el balcón = *balcony*

Useful vocabulary

la foto	*photo*	**el armario**	*cupboard / wardrobe*
el dormitorio	*bedroom*	**la puerta**	*door*
la cama	*bed*	**los estantes**	*shelves*
la silla	*chair*	**el ordenador**	*computer*
la luz	*light*	**la cortina**	*curtain*
la mesa	*table / desk*	**la alfombra**	*carpet / rug*
la ventana	*window*		

3. What is in this photo?
Write **five** sentences in **Spanish**.

+ Remember

You can use the verb **hay** *there is / there are* but, for variety, you could also say **El dormitorio tiene ...** *The bedroom has ...*, **La cama está al lado de ...** *The bed is next to ...* You could also mention some colours but the photos in the exam will be black and white.

Note this construction:
¿Desde cuándo vives en tu casa? *How long have you lived in your house?*
Vivo en mi / esta casa desde hace cuatro años.
I have lived in my / this house for four years.

Role play

TRACK 76

4. Plan what you are going to say in this role play, taking into account the number of details you will need. Then play the recording, pausing after each question or statement so you can give your response.
(This is in the style of a Higher tier role play).

4.1 Say what your house is like. (Give **two** details.)
4.2 Say how long you have lived there. (Give **one** detail.)
4.3 Say what you think of your bedroom and why. (Give **one** opinion and **one** reason.)
4.4 Say what your ideal house would be like. (Give **two** details.)
? 4.5 Ask your friend a question about where they live.

★ You could use **Me gustaría tener ...** and then mention what you would like to have in your house.

TOWNS AND CITIES

En la ciudad   *In town*

1. Listen to these five people talking.
   Which **three** things does each person have in their town?

TRACK 77

A	bank
B	bridge
C	café
D	cinema
E	factory

F	hospital
G	library
H	market
I	park
J	river

K	school
L	shopping centre
M	shops
N	stadium
O	train station

1.1 E, C, N   1.2 F, H, M   1.3 L, D, I   1.4 K, B, J   1.5 G, A, O

Talking about where things are

cerca (de)	*near / close (to)*
al final (de)	*at the end of*
antes (de)	*before*
delante (de)	*in front of*

lejos (de)	*far (from)*
al lado (de)	*next to*
después (de)	*after*
detrás (de)	*behind*

2. Reply to these questions, using the information in brackets.

Example | ¿Sabes dónde está el mercado? | (It's at the end of the street.) Está al final de la calle.

2.1 | Por favor, ¿dónde está el banco? | (It's not far, in front of the library.)

2.2 | ¿Sabes dónde está el cine? | (It's very near, before the river.)

2.3 | ¿Por dónde se va al hospital? | (It's after the cinema, next to the park.)

2.4 | Por favor, ¿dónde está la estación? | (It's at the end of the street, behind the stadium.)

2.5 | ¿Dónde está el café? | (It's quite far, close to the river.)

2.1 No está lejos, (está) delante de la biblioteca.
2.2 Está muy cerca, antes del río.
2.3 Está después del cine, al lado del parque.
2.4 Está al final de la calle, detrás del estadio.
2.5 Está bastante lejos, cerca del río.

¿Qué hay en tu pueblo / tu ciudad?

A positive response

Mi ciudad es muy bonita y es muy popular con los turistas porque es histórica, y es famosa por su arquitectura preciosa y edificios hermosos. El barrio antiguo tiene unas tiendas tradicionales y restaurantes agradables. En la zona moderna están los bancos y el centro comercial. Me encanta mi ciudad y no viviría en ningún otro sitio.

Alejandro

A negative response

Mi ciudad me aburre un montón porque no hay nada que hacer para los jóvenes. Es un lugar viejo y, en el pasado, había mucha industria y varias fábricas. En mi opinión, es una ciudad fea donde siempre hace mal tiempo. Para ir al cine o a las tiendas de moda, tenemos que coger el autobús para ir a la ciudad cercana. Preferiría vivir en otro sitio.

Julia

3. Answer the questions in **English**.

3.1 What is Alejandro's town famous for?

3.2 Where can the traditional shops be found?

3.3 What is there in the modern district?

3.4 Why is Julia bored with her town?

3.5 What did the town have in the past?

3.6 What opinion does she give of her town?

3.7 What do Julia and her friends do if they want to go to the cinema?

3.1 *beautiful architecture and lovely buildings*
3.2 *in the old quarter / district*
3.3 *banks and a shopping centre*
3.4 *There is nothing to do for young people.*
3.5 *(a lot of) industry and (several) factories*
3.6 *It is ugly and the weather is always bad.*
3.7 *catch the bus to the nearby town / city*

To give a full answer to five of these seven questions, you will need to give two details. If you give only one detail, you will not have provided a full answer and cannot be awarded the mark for the question. The question will always say if it requires detail.

DESCRIBING THE AREA

En mi región   *In my area*

¿Dónde prefieres vivir – en la ciudad o en el campo?

Where do you prefer to live – in the town or in the country?

Look at these phrases you can use to express your preference.

Prefiero **la ciudad** porque ... *I prefer the town / city because...*		Prefiero **el campo** porque ... *I prefer the country because...*	
hay mucho que hacer	*there's lots to do*	es muy tranquilo	*it's very peaceful*
es muy animado	*it's very lively*	el aire es puro	*the air is pure*
es fácil ir al cine	*it's easy to go to the cinema*	la vida es más lenta	*life is slower*
estás cerca de las tiendas	*you're near the shops*	hay mucho espacio	*there's lots of space*
hay un ambiente divertido	*there's a fun atmosphere*	no hay ruido	*there's no noise*

✚ Remember

If you are writing about the past ...   **hay → había** *there was / there were*   **es → era** *it was*
está(s) → estaba(s) *it was / (you were)*   **me gusta(n) → me gustaba(n)** *I liked it (them)*

---

1. Read what the local people are posting on the council website about the area.
   Which aspects are getting positive feedback (**P**), and which are getting negative
   comments (**N**)?

   ⊕ Aprecio los espacios verdes que hay. Gracias al ayuntamiento por cuidar los árboles en la plaza.

   ⊗ La falta de un sitio para dejar el coche en la ciudad significa que menos personas visitan mi tienda en la Calle Mayor.

   ⊕ Con la nueva estación de autobuses, es mucho más fácil llegar al trabajo y salir de excursión.

   ⊗ La cantidad de basura en el camino al lado del río y en el pueblo es horrible. Las calles no están limpias.

   ⊕ Aquí tenemos campo bonito y paisajes impresionantes. Debemos estar orgullosos de nuestra región.

   ⊗ El tráfico en el centro es peligroso y ruidoso. Hace falta una carretera que quite los coches del centro.

1.1	cleanliness	**1.3**	parking situation	**1.5**	traffic
1.2	green spaces	**1.4**	surrounding area	**1.6**	transport links

   1.1 N   1.2 P   1.3 N   1.4 P   1.5 N   1.6 P

Expressing positive and negative opinions

Look at these ways of expressing the good and the bad about your area:

lo bueno de ...	*the good thing about ...*	lo malo de ...	*the bad thing about ...*
lo mejor de ...	*the best thing about ...*	lo peor de ...	*the worst thing about ...*
lo que más me gusta es ...	*what I like best is ...*	lo que menos me gusta es ...	*what I like least is ...*

2. ❶ Translate these sentences into **Spanish**.

2.1 What I like best about my town are the pretty squares and the green spaces.

2.2 The worst thing about my town is the traffic. It is dangerous near the school.

2.3 The good thing about my town is that the transport system is excellent.

2.4 I am proud of my area. It has green countryside and lovely scenery.

2.5 What I like least about my area is the litter. The streets are not very clean.

2.1 Lo que más me gusta de mi ciudad son las plazas bonitas y los espacios verdes.
2.2 Lo peor de mi ciudad es el tráfico. Es peligroso cerca del instituto.
2.3 Lo bueno de mi ciudad es que el sistema de transporte es excelente.
2.4 Estoy orgulloso/a de mi región. Tiene campo verde y paisajes hermosos.
2.5 Lo que menos me gusta de mi región es la basura. Las calles no están muy limpias.

3. ❶ Imagine you used to live in the city and now live in the country. Write about your impressions of both. (This is a Higher tier style of writing task.)

Write approximately **150 words** in **Spanish**.

You must write something about both bullet points.

Mention:
- what you liked and did not like about living in the city
- what you like and do not like about living in the country.

Example response

> *Me gustaba vivir en la ciudad porque era muy agradable y había un ambiente divertido. Era fácil ir a las tiendas o al cine, porque todo estaba cerca de mi casa y el sistema de transporte era excelente. Siempre había mucho que hacer y nunca estaba aburrido. Sin embargo, había mucho tráfico y bastante contaminación del aire. No había mucho espacio y las calles estaban llenas de gente. Ahora vivo en el campo y me gustan mucho los árboles verdes y los paisajes hermosos. La vida aquí es más lenta y el aire es más puro. Las calles están limpias porque hay menos personas y poco tráfico. Es un estilo de vida tranquilo y sin ruido de los coches. Por otro lado, puede ser un poco aburrido porque no hay mucho que hacer, aparte de dar paseos, y todos mis amigos todavía viven en la ciudad. ¡Creo que me gustaría volver a la ciudad!* **[154 words]**

THE ENVIRONMENT

You see this list of advice reminding people what they can do to help the environment.

1. Read the advice then find the following **-ar** verbs and write them in the infinitive:

1.1 to take / carry _____

1.2 to turn off _____

1.3 to grow _____

1.4 to separate _____

1.5 to reuse _____

1.6 to use _____

1.7 to plant _____

1.8 to recycle _____

1.9 to save _____

- Hay que mantener las calles limpias – lleva tu basura a casa.
- Separa la basura y ponla en los contenedores correctos.
- Recicla todo lo que puedes.
- Ahorra agua.
- Cultiva tus propias verduras.
- Planta árboles.
- Reutiliza el plástico que usas.
- Utiliza el transporte público.
- Apaga la luz cuando sales de la habitación.

1.1 to take / carry – llevar, 1.2 to turn off – apagar, 1.3 to grow – cultivar,
1.4 to separate – separar, 1.5 to reuse – reutilizar, 1.6 to use – utilizar,
1.7 to plant – plantar, 1.8 to recycle – reciclar, 1.9 to save – ahorrar

2. To practise saying what you did last week, translate these short sentences into **Spanish** using the first person of the preterite tense.

2.1 I planted a tree.

2.2 I recycled bottles.

2.3 I saved water.

2.4 I took the rubbish home.

2.5 I separated the rubbish.

2.6 I turned off the lights.

2.7 I reused a plastic bottle.

2.8 I used public transport.

2.1. Planté un árbol. 2.2. Reciclé botellas. 2.3. Ahorré agua. 2.4. Llevé la basura a casa.
2.5. Separé la basura. 2.6. Apagué las luces. 2.7. Reutilicé una botella de plástico.
2.8. Utilicé el transporte público.

! Be careful with the irregular verbs that end in **-gar** and **-zar**.

The yo part of a **-gar** verb ends in **-gué** in the preterite.
e.g. **llegar → llegué**

The **yo** part of a **-zar** verb ends in **-cé** in the preterite.
e.g. **empezar → empecé**

3. Now listen to these four students talking about environmental projects in their high school. What does each school's environmental project consist of?

TRACK 78

Write the answers in **English**.

3.1. *They are going to collect and recycle all the plastic bottles used in school.*
3.2. *They are creating a garden on the sports field to grow fruit and veg.*
3.3. *A group of students is responsible for turning off lights and computers at the end of the day.*
3.4. *They had a 'no-car day' and everyone had either to walk, cycle or use public transport.*

Giving commands

When you are telling someone to do something, you use the part of the verb called the imperative. For regular verbs, it is the same as the he/she/it form of the verb. See **page 156**.

| eg | **¡Espera!** *Wait!* |

| eg | **¡Corre!** *Run!*   **¡Escribe!** *Write!* |

!   Note the irregulars: **di** *say/tell*, **haz** *do/make*, **pon** *put*, **sal** *leave/go out*, **ve** *go*, **ven** *come*.

4. Translate these commands into **English**.

4.1 Ahorra el agua de la lluvia.
4.2 Apaga la televisión.
4.3 Ayuda al medio ambiente.
4.4 Coge el autobús.
4.5 Utiliza tu bicicleta.
4.6 Di la verdad.
4.7 Pon la basura en el contenedor.
4.8 Describe el problema.

4.1 *Save rainwater.*
4.2 *Turn off the television.*
4.3 *Help the environment.*
4.4 *Catch the bus.*
4.5 *Use your bike.*
4.6 *Tell the truth.*
4.7 *Put the rubbish in the bin.*
4.8 *Describe the problem.*

5. ❽ Read this passage aloud and then check your pronunciation by listening to the recording.

TRACK 79

Then answer the four recorded questions.

La semana pasada, en el pueblo, tuvimos un día dedicado al medio ambiente. Recogimos toda la basura en las calles y evitamos usar los coches. En la escuela, los niños cultivaron verduras en el jardín y plantaron árboles en el parque. Yo apagué las luces en el instituto al final del día.

THE GLOBAL ENVIRONMENT

Temas globales   *Global issues*

1. Ⓗ Read this article about environmental issues and answer the questions below.

> El cambio climático significa que el planeta está cambiando y esto no solo afecta a los animales y la naturaleza sino a la gente también. Algunas especies están amenazadas y, si perdemos una especie de insectos, por ejemplo, entonces estarán en peligro los pájaros que comen esos insectos y dependen de ellos para sobrevivir.
>
> También, los animales sufren por una falta de hábitat porque nosotros, los seres humanos, seguimos destrozando las zonas donde viven. Cortamos los bosques para crear más zonas para la agricultura sin pensar en los impactos en el equilibrio de la naturaleza. Se dice que, algún día en el futuro, algunas zonas de la tierra o estarán bajo agua (porque el nivel del mar está subiendo) o estarán demasiado calientes para ser habitadas.

1.1   According to the article, what three things are affected by climate change?

1.2   What could happen if a certain type of insect becomes extinct?

1.3   What else, as well as the climate, is endangering animals?

1.4   What are people doing in order to create space for agriculture?

1.5   What should they be bearing in mind?

1.6   Why might areas be flooded in the future?

1.7   Why else might certain areas be uninhabitable for humans?

1.1   animals, nature and people
1.2   The birds that depend on them for food could become endangered.
1.3   lack / destruction of habitat
1.4   cutting down forests
1.5   the impact on the balance of nature
1.6   Sea levels are rising.
1.7   They will be too hot.

¿Qué se debe hacer para resolver los problemas medioambientales?

Hay que cultivar más bosques.

Tenemos que proteger la naturaleza.

Reduce, reutiliza, recicla.

Se debe comer menos carne.

Crea un jardín para la naturaleza.

Debemos usar menos energía.

Podríamos dejar el coche en casa.

Hace falta usar energías más limpias.

Se podría volar menos.

2. Read the recommendations, work out what they mean and find the following expressions:

2.1 we have to / must (**two** expressions)

2.2 you / one must

2.3 you / one could

2.4 it is necessary (**two** expressions)

2.5 we could

2.6 create

2.7 to fly

2.8 cleaner energies

2.1 tenemos que / debemos
2.2 se debe
2.3 se podría
2.4 hay que / hace falta
2.5 podríamos
2.6 crea
2.7 volar
2.8 energías más limpias

THE ENVIRONMENT AND WHERE PEOPLE LIVE

Ponerlo todo junto *Putting it all together*

1.  Read what Emma and Hugo say about where they live.
   Who mentions these aspects? Emma (**E**), Hugo (**H**) or Emma and Hugo (**E + H**)?

Vivo en un pueblo en el norte de España en la costa y es una zona hermosa con montañas y paisajes hermosos. Es una región muy verde porque tenemos más lluvia que otras partes del país. En las ciudades, hay problemas con los humos de las fábricas y los coches, pero es fácil dejar atrás la ciudad para escapar al campo y al aire limpio. Vivo aquí desde hace siete años y creo que es el mejor sitio del mundo. **Emma**

Vivo en la costa sur de España en una zona turística. Es una región muy bonita con pueblos blancos de casas típicas y flores rojas en los balcones. Sin embargo, al lado de la playa hay zonas muy feas de enormes hoteles y atracciones para los turistas. En mi opinión, han destrozado la zona con demasiada construcción. Aquí notamos el cambio climático cada año más, con temperaturas altísimas. **Hugo**

1.1 the weather	1.3 natural scenery	1.5 how long they have lived there
1.2 air pollution	1.4 traditional homes	1.6 the impact of visitors to the area

1.1 E + H   1.2 E   1.3 E   1.4 H   1.5 E   1.6 H

2. You are in Spain visiting your friend, Martín. His mother is showing you around the flat. Listen to what she says.

   TRACK 80

   Select the correct option to complete the sentences in each question.

   2.1 You will **stay in a university residence / have to share a room / have your own room.**

   David is **Martín's brother / staying with a friend / a university lecturer.**

   2.2 The bedroom is missing a **cupboard / chair / table.**

   The missing item is currently in the **kitchen / dining room / lounge.**

   2.3 The bathroom is **at the end of the corridor / next to your room / opposite Martín's room.**

   2.4 They take their meals **in the dining room / on their knees in the lounge / at the kitchen table.**

   2.1 have your own room / Martín's brother   2.2 chair / lounge
   2.3 next to your room   2.4 at the kitchen table

Photo card

3. Look at the two photos and prepare ideas on what to say about them. Remember to say something about both photos and to talk for one minute (**F**) or one and a half minutes (**H**). Then listen to the recording to hear an example of what could be said.

TRACK 81

Photo 1

Photo 2

4. **H** Translate these sentences into **Spanish**.

4.1 My favourite room in the house is my bedroom because it is comfortable and peaceful.

4.2 There was a library behind the town hall, but now it is closed.

4.3 What I like best about my town is that there is a lot to do for young people.

4.4 We picked up the litter on the sports field and I helped to plant some trees.

4.5 We must look after the forests and protect our threatened species.

4.1 *Mi habitación favorita en la casa es mi dormitorio porque es cómodo y tranquilo.*

4.2 *Había una biblioteca detrás del ayuntamiento, pero ahora está cerrada.*

4.3 *Lo que más me gusta de mi ciudad es que hay mucho que hacer para los jóvenes.*

4.4 *Recogimos la basura en el campo de deportes y ayudé a plantar unos / algunos árboles.*

4.5 *Tenemos que / Debemos cuidar los bosques y proteger nuestras especies amenazadas.*

KEY VOCABULARY

Students are expected to know 1200 items of vocabulary for Foundation tier and a further 500 for Higher tier. This list has some of the key vocabulary for Theme 3, but there are many more words listed in the AQA specification and in an interactive spreadsheet on the AQA website.

bonito	pretty, nice
limpio	clean
sucio	dirty
la basura	rubbish, junk
la casa	house
la ciudad	city, town
el pueblo	village, small town
el campo	countryside
el medioambiente	environment
contaminar	to pollute, contaminate
vivir	to live
fácil	easy
la pantalla	screen, monitor
el mensaje	message
el móvil	mobile phone
el videojuego	computer game
compartir	to share
bajar	to download, go down
enviar / mandar	to send
la tableta	tablet (eg. iPad)
el ordenador	computer
el seguidor	follower
hace calor	it's hot
hace frío	it's cold
la playa	beach
la estación	station, season (of the year)
las vacaciones, de vacaciones	holiday, on holiday
el aeropuerto	airport
el avión	plane, aeroplane
el metro	underground, tube
el tren	train
el coche	car
viajar	to travel
el/la turista	tourist

EXAMINATION PRACTICE

Communication and the world around us — Reading

These people have written their comments on their town's web page.

×

01 Olivia
Desde que mejoraron el centro y construyeron las nuevas zonas libres de coches, me parece que la ciudad es un buen sitio para vivir.

02 Rodrigo
Los espacios verdes que han creado están bien. Los barrios pobres están muy sucios y todavía hay mucho que hacer.

03 Martina
En mi opinión, en esta ciudad hay muy pocas actividades para los jóvenes. Otra cosa es que tengo miedo si estoy a solas en la calle porque faltan luces.

04 Manolo
La verdad es que yo he viajado mucho con mi familia y siempre tengo ganas de volver aquí, a la ciudad donde nací. No hay otra ciudad como ésta.

What do they think about the town? Write **P** for a **positive** opinion, **N** for a **negative** opinion, **P + N** for a **positive and negative** opinion. [4 marks]

01 Olivia: _____ 02 Rodrigo: _____ 03 Martina: _____ 04 Manolo: _____

H You read this article about ideas for different holidays.

> Si haces camping como familia es una buena oportunidad para trabajar en equipo y hacer actividades juntos.
>
> Pasar un par de semanas en una casa de campo en una zona rural de España te ayuda a ponerte en contacto con la naturaleza y olvidarte de las tensiones de la vida urbana.
>
> Hay mucho interés en las vacaciones de trabajo voluntario como construir una escuela o ayudar con proyectos medioambientales. Muchas relaciones han empezado aquí y algunos participantes terminaron casándose.
>
> Ir a la costa en julio y agosto es un error grave porque no tendrás la energía para hacer visitas o excursiones. Con el calor que hace no tendrás interés en nada aparte de buscar la sombra.

Answer the following questions in **English**.

05 What are the benefits of camping as a family? [2 marks]

06 What can a holiday in the country help you to do? [2 marks]

07 What **two** types of voluntary work are mentioned? [2 marks]

08 What do we learn about some of the volunteers? [1 mark]

09 What is the drawback of holidaying on the coast in summer? [1 mark]

10 What do people end up doing in July and August? [1 mark]

Communication and the world around us – Listening

Ⓗ These four people are calling a radio phone-in about new technology.

What are their opinions? Write **P** for a **positive** opinion, **N** for a **negative** opinion and **P + N** for a **positive and negative** opinion.

TRACK 82

01 First speaker: _____ [1 mark]

02 Second speaker: _____ [1 mark]

03 Third speaker: _____ [1 mark]

04 Fourth speaker: _____ [1 mark]

Hugo is phoning his grandfather to tell him about his week. Write the correct **number** for Hugo's activity. Write the correct **letter** for when it takes place.

TRACK 83

	Activity			When
1	Revising	P	Past
2	Sunbathing	N	Now
3	Watching a film	F	Future
4	Working		

05 Activity: _____   When: _____ [2 marks]

06 Activity: _____   When: _____ [2 marks]

Ⓗ Dictation

07 You will now hear **five** short sentences.

TRACK 84

Listen carefully and, using your knowledge of Spanish sounds, write down in **Spanish** exactly what you hear for each sentence.

You will hear each sentence **three** times: the first time as a full sentence, the second time in short sections and the third time again as a full sentence.

Use your knowledge of Spanish sounds and grammar to make sure that what you have written makes sense. Check carefully that your spelling is accurate.

(Note that, on the Foundation **Ⓕ** paper, there are only four sentences.) [10 marks]

Communication and the world around us – Speaking

🄷 Role play

Plan what you are going to say in this role play, taking into account the number of details you will need. Remember to use a verb in each response. Then play the recording, pausing after each question or statement so you can give your response. (This is in the style of a Higher tier role play). When you see this **–?–** you will have to ask a question.

TRACK 85

[10 marks]

01 You are talking to your Cuban friend.

    01.1 Say where you usually go on holiday and why. (Give **one** place.)

    01.2 Say how you used technology to plan your holiday. (Give **two** details.)

    01.3 Say how you prefer to travel and why. (Give **one** method of transport and **one** reason.)

    01.4 Say what you do with friends during the summer holidays. (Give **two** details.)

?   01.5 Ask your friend about the place where they live.

---

02 🄷 **Read aloud** the following passage and then answer the questions in the recording. This is a Higher tier task.

[5 + 10 marks]

> Cuando estoy de vacaciones con mi familia, nos divertimos juntos y hacemos muchas actividades diferentes. Es genial porque mis padres pagan todo. Cada año, compro recuerdos para mis amigos y los llamo a veces para preguntar qué están haciendo. Volver a casa al final de la semana es horrible.

TRACK 86

Photo card

03 Look at the two photos and prepare ideas on what to say about them. Remember to say something about both photos and to talk for **one minute** (🄵) or **one and a half minutes** (🄷).

[5 marks]

Photo 1

Photo 2

TRACK 87

04 Now answer the recorded questions for the unprepared conversation on the theme. [20 marks]

Communication and the world around us – Writing

01 Translate the following sentences into **Spanish**. [10 marks]

(This is aimed at top ❻ to ❽ level.)

01.1 I used the computer to book the flights.

01.2 María helps her grandfather to do his shopping online.

01.3 He was doing his homework on his laptop.

01.4 Young people spend too much time on their mobile phones.

01.5 I forgot to save my work.

02 You are writing an article about home and travel.

Write approximately **90 words** in **Spanish**. You must write something about each bullet point.

(This is a ❻ and ❽ task.) [15 marks]

Mention:
- what you think about the area where you live
- what you did during the last holidays
- where you would most like to travel.

03 You are writing a post for a website about the environment.

Write approximately **150 words** in **Spanish**. You must write something about both bullet points.

(This is a ❽ task.) [25 marks]

Mention:
- why you are concerned about environmental problems
- what you are going to do in your school to help the environment.

GRAMMAR

The grammar requirements for GCSE are set out in two tiers: Foundation and Higher.

Students are required to use their knowledge of grammar from the specified lists, appropriate to the relevant tier of entry.

Students completing Higher tier assessments will be required to apply all grammar listed for Foundation tier in addition to the grammar listed for ⓗ Higher tier.

NOUNS AND ARTICLES

Nouns

Nouns are words used to name a thing, person or place. Examples: 'book', 'teacher', 'house'. It often helps to ask yourself if a word can have 'the' before it. If it can, it is a noun ('the book', 'the teacher', 'the house').

Spanish nouns all have a gender: they are either masculine or feminine.

Masculine nouns

Masculine nouns usually end in **-o**:
libro *book*, **año** *year*, **abuelo** *grandfather*

But other endings also exist:
cine *cinema*, **color** *colour*, **avión** *plane*, **móvil** *mobile*

Feminine nouns

Feminine nouns mostly end in **-a**:
novela *novel*, **playa** *beach*, **hermana** *sister*

But there are also other endings:
madre *mother*, **pared** *wall*, **voz** *voice*

Nouns ending in **-ante**, **-ente** and **-ista**, which represent people, can be either masculine or feminine.

el estudiante → *male student*   **la estudiante** → *female student*

los estudiantes → *male students* OR *students in general*

el artista → *male artist*   **la artista** → *female artist*

los artistas → *male artists* OR *artists in general*

Words ending in **-dad** are feminine:
la verdad *truth*, **la universidad** *university*, **la edad** *age*

Words ending in **-ión** (except **avión**) are feminine: **la canción** *song*, **la televisión** *television*

Some common words ending in **-ma** are masculine: **el idioma** *language*, **el problema** *problem*

! Some common exceptions: **el día** *day*, **la mano** *hand*, **la foto** *photo*, **el planeta** *planet*

+ Remember

Adding **-ito** or **-ita** to a noun means it is small or implies affection:

hermanito *little brother*
gatito *kitten*

Using the infinitive as a noun

In English we use the '-ing' part of the verb as a noun, for example: 'Smoking is bad for your health.'

In Spanish, the infinitive is used instead:
Fumar es malo para la salud.

It is treated as a masculine noun.

Plurals of nouns

If a noun ends in a vowel (**a**, **e**, **i**, **o**, **u**), add an **-s** to make the plural.

| eg | chico → chicos *boys*   zona → zonas *areas*   puente → puentes *bridges* |

If a noun ends in any other letter, add **-es** to make the plural.

| eg | plan → planes *plans*   flor → flores *flowers*   árbol → árboles *trees* |

Exception: if a noun ends in **-z**, then the **z** changes to **c** before you add **-es**.

| eg | voz → voces *voices*   luz → luces *lights*   disfraz → disfraces *costumes* |

| ! | When a noun ends in **-ín**, **-ión** or **-ón**, the accent disappears in the plural:
jardín → **jardines** *gardens*   **acción** → **acciones** *actions*   **montón** → **montones** *loads* |

Articles

There are two types of **articles**. The definite article in English is 'the', and the indefinite articles are 'a', 'an' and 'some'.

Both the definite and the indefinite article depend on the gender and number of the noun:

Definite articles

masculine singular	masculine plural	feminine singular	feminine plural
el	los	la	las
el coche *the car*	los gatos *the cats*	la oficina *the office*	las casas *the houses*

Indefinite articles

masculine singular	masculine plural	feminine singular	feminine plural
un	unos	una	unas
un coche *a car*	unos gatos *some cats*	una oficina *an office*	unas casas *some houses*

| ! | Unlike in English, the definite article is used in Spanish to indicate when you are generalising:
La igualdad es esencial. *Equality is essential.*
The definite article in Spanish is omitted after **ser** when followed by an occupation / profession:
Mi hermana es profesora. *My sister is a teacher.* |

 Remember

Remember that **a** + **el** shortens to **al**, and **de** + **el** shortens to **del**.

ADJECTIVES

Adjectives

In Spanish, adjectives have different endings that change depending on which noun they describe. Therefore, they have endings to match masculine, feminine, singular and plural nouns. In Spanish, most adjectives go after the noun.

The masculine singular form usually ends in **-o**.

masculine singular	masculine plural	feminine singular	feminine plural
-o	-os	-a	-as
alt**o**	alt**os**	alt**a**	alt**as**

Mi madre es baja. *My mother is short.*   **Tengo dos gatos blancos.** *I have two white cats.*

Some adjectives end in **-e** in the singular form. These have one singular form and one plural form.

masculine singular	masculine plural	feminine singular	feminine plural
-e	-es	-e	-es
alegr**e**	alegr**es**	alegr**e**	alegr**es**

noticias recientes *recent news*   **un ambiente alegre** *a happy atmosphere*

Adjectives that end in any consonant (e.g. **-r**, **-l**, **-s**) do not change in the feminine form.

masculine singular	masculine plural	feminine singular	feminine plural
-l	-les	-l	-les
azu**l**	azu**les**	azu**l**	azu**les**

la camiseta azul *the blue T-shirt*   **Tengo los ojos azules.** *I have blue eyes.*

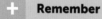 **Remember**

If an adjective describes a masculine and a feminine noun, then the masculine plural form is used:
David y María son muy simpáticos y alegres.
David and Maria are very nice and cheerful.

! When an adjective ends in **-z**, change the **-z** to a **-c** before adding **-es**.
feliz → felices *happy*

Adjectives of nationality

masculine singular	masculine plural	feminine singular	feminine plural
-o cuban**o**	-os cuban**os**	-a cuban**a**	-as cuban**as**
-l español	-les españo**les**	-la español**a**	-las español**as**
-és franc**és**	-eses franc**eses**	-esa franc**esa**	-esas franc**esas**
-án alem**án**	-anes alem**anes**	-ana alem**ana**	-anas alem**anas**

> **!** Note that adjectives of nationality do not have capital letters.

Adjectives that change their meaning depending on position

These **adjectives** have a different meaning depending on whether they come before or after the noun.

Before		After	
mi antigua casa	*my old (former) house*	una casa antigua	*an old house*
ciertas personas	*certain people*	una cosa cierta	*a sure thing*
un gran hombre	*a great man*	un hombre grande	*a big man*
la pobre mujer	*the poor woman (feeling sorry)*	una mujer pobre	*a poor woman (financially)*
una situación única	*a unique situation*	la única vez	*the only time*

Adjectives with ser and estar

Some adjectives have different meanings depending on whether they are with ser or estar.

Ser		Estar	
ser listo/a	*to be clever / intelligent*	estar listo/a	*to be ready / prepared*
ser bueno/a	*to be good (kind / nice)*	estar bueno/a	*to be good (of food – tasty / delicious)*
ser malo/a	*to be bad (person / quality)*	estar malo/a	*to be ill / unwell*
ser rico/a	*to be rich / well-off*	estar rico/a	*to be delicious (of food)*
ser aburrido/a	*to be boring*	estar aburrido/a	*to be bored*

Demonstrative adjectives

These correspond to the English 'this', 'these', 'that' and 'those'. The Spanish equivalents go before the noun.

This	
masculine singular **este**	feminine singular **esta**

These	
masculine singular **estos**	feminine singular **estas**

That (not far)	
masculine singular **ese**	feminine singular **esa**

Those (not far)	
masculine singular **esos**	feminine singular **esas**

Ⓗ That (over there)	
masculine singular **aquel**	feminine singular **aquella**

Ⓗ Those (over there)	
masculine singular **aquellos**	feminine singular **aquellas**

este regalo *this present*   **esta maleta** *this suitcase*   **esos tomates** *those tomatoes*

estas mochilas *these rucksacks*   **aquel puente** *that bridge*   **aquellas montañas** *those mountains*

> **!** Note the neutral forms **esto** *this* and **eso** *that* when no gender is implied.
>
> Example: **Tengo que pensar en eso.** *I have to think about that.*
> **¿Qué es esto?** *What is this?*
>
> Ⓗ **aquello** (neutral) – *that (over there)*

Indefinite adjectives

These are listed separately because, unlike most adjectives, they go before the noun. See **page 85**.

Adjective		Example		Notes
mismo	*same*	la misma palabra	*the same word*	
otro	*other / another*	el otro día otra oportunidad	*the other day* *another opportunity*	no indefinite article (**un / una**) before
todo	*all / every*	toda la semana todas las personas	*all week* *all the people*	definite article (**el, la, los, las**) always used before the following noun
alguno	*some*	algún día algunas ideas	*someday* *some ideas*	**alguno** shortens to **algún** before a masculine singular noun
ninguno	*none / not any*	ningún dinero ninguna casa	*no money* *no houses*	**ninguno** shortens to **ningún** before a masculine singular noun
cada	*each / every*	cada día	*each / every day*	**cada** is invariable (never changes)

Possessive adjectives

These are adjectives like 'my', 'your' and 'our' that indicate possession or ownership. In Spanish they go before the noun.

English	Spanish	Examples
my	mi / mis	**mi amigo** *my friend*, **mis padres** *my parents*
your (referring to singular you)	tu / tus	**tu casa** *your house*, **tus ideas** *your ideas*
his / her / its your (formal)	su / sus	**su perro** *his / her / your dog*, **sus mensajes** *his / her / your messages*
our	nuestro / -a / -os / -as	**nuestra profesora** *our teacher*, **nuestros libros** *our books*
your (referring to plural you)	vuestro / -a / -os / -as	**vuestro jardín** *your garden*, **vuestras opiniones** *your opinions*
your (formal)	su / sus	**su piso** *their / your flat*, **sus hijos** *their / your children*

 These possessive adjectives agree with the **following noun**.

The shortening of adjectives (apocopation)

Certain adjectives go before the noun and, when they are with a masculine singular noun, they lose their final **-o**. **Grande** shortens before both masculine and feminine singular nouns.

primero → primer	**el primer día** *(on) the first day*
tercero → tercer	**el tercer libro** *the third book*
alguno → algún	**algún riesgo** *some risk*
ninguno → ningún	**en ningún momento** *at no time*
bueno → buen	**Es un buen hombre.** *He's a good man.*
malo → mal	**Hace muy mal tiempo.** *The weather is really bad.*
grande → gran	**Vamos a tener una gran fiesta.** *We're going to have a great party.*

 These adjectives agree as usual with plural nouns and feminine singular nouns: **la primera semana**, **algunas ideas**

Comparatives and superlatives

These are adjectival phrases that show you are making a comparison: 'more expensive than', 'cleaner', 'as tall as', 'less difficult', etc. The adjectives in the phrases agree with the noun as normal.

Comparatives

more ... than →	más ... que	**Juan es más alto que Pedro.** *Juan is taller than Pedro. (Literally 'more tall than')*
less ... than →	menos ... que	**Este ejercicio es menos difícil que el otro.** *This exercise is less difficult than the other one.*
as ... as →	tan ... como	**Murcia es tan grande como Bilbao.** *Murcia is as big as Bilbao.*
as much / many ... as →	tanto /-a /-os /-as -como	**No tengo tantos deberes como tú.** *I haven't got as much homework as you.*

> **!** When 'more / less than' is followed by a number, **de** is used for 'than'.
> **Invitaron a más de cien personas**. *They invited more than a hundred people.*

ⓗ Superlatives

the most, the -est →	el / la / los / las más	**Esta camiseta es la más apropiada.** *This T-shirt is the most suitable.*
the least →	el / la / los / las menos	**Estos zapatos son los menos caros.** *These shoes are the least expensive.*

Note the irregulars:

better	→ mejor	best	→	el / la mejor, los / las mejores
worse	→ peor	worst	→	el / la peor, los / las peores
older / bigger	→ mayor	oldest / biggest	→	el / la mayor, los / las mayores
younger / smaller	→ menor	youngest / smallest	→	el / la menor, los / las menores

> **!** When 'in' follows a superlative ('the tallest **in** the country'), use **de**.
> **Este edificio es el más alto del país.** *This building is the tallest in the country.*

ADVERBS

These are words that describe how the action of a verb is being done, such as 'carefully', 'slowly', 'often', 'fast'. They can also be used with an adjective: 'It was really delicious.'

Many Spanish adverbs are formed by adding **-mente** to the feminine singular form of the adjective.

masculine adjective	feminine adjective	adverb	
rápido	rápida	rápidamente	*quickly*
probable	probable	probablemente	*probably*
feliz	feliz	felizmente	*happily*

! Some common adverbs are irregular.

well → **bien**
badly → **mal**
better → **mejor**
worse → **peor**

Adverbs of time

hoy *today*		mañana *tomorrow*	ayer *yesterday*
pasado mañana *the day after tomorrow*		ahora *now*	ya *now / already*

Adverbs of frequency

a veces *sometimes*	muchas veces *often*	frecuentemente *frequently*
siempre *always*	raramente *rarely*	

Adverbs of sequence

antes *before*	después *then / afterwards*	luego *next*	entonces *then / so*

Adverbs of place

dentro de *inside*	fuera de *outside*	aquí *here*
cerca *near*	lejos *far*	allí *there*

Quantifiers and intensifiers

bastante *enough / quite*	mucho *a lot*	un poco *a little / a bit*
demasiado *too / too much*	muy *very*	poco *little / not much*

PRONOUNS

Subject pronouns

Subject pronouns are the words that refer to the person or thing doing the action of the verb. In English, they are found before the verb. For example: '**He** is making the dinner.' '**We** are watching a film.' '**It** is not working.'

yo	*I*	nosotros / nosotras	*we*
tú	*you (s)*	vosotros / vosotras	*you (pl)*
él	*he / it (m)*	ellos	*they (m)*
ella	*she / it (f)*	ellas	*they (f)*
usted	*you (formal s)*	ustedes	*you (formal pl)*

In Spanish they are used a lot less than in English because the verb ending tells us who / what is doing the action of the verb. They are used for emphasis, or clarification if there is any ambiguity or confusion.

Mis amigas van al concierto mañana, pero yo no voy. No me gusta ese tipo de música.

*My friends are going to the concert tomorrow, but **I'm** not going. I don't like that type of music.*

Mis hermanos, Ana y Leo, están en la universidad. Ella estudia medicina y él estudia derecho.

My brother and sister, Ana and Leo, are at university. She is studying medicine and he is studying law.

Tú and usted

Normally you use **tú** and the second person singular of the verb when talking to one person, and **vosotros/-as** with the second person plural of the verb when talking to more than one person.

Use **usted** with the third person singular of the verb if you feel you need to be extra respectful and polite (talking to a Spanish friend's grandmother, or the headteacher in a Spanish school, for example). **Ustedes** is the formal plural form and goes with the third person plural of the verb.

Usted is often shortened to **Ud.** or **Vd.** **Ustedes** abbreviates to **Uds.** or **Vds.**

Direct object pronouns

These are the pronouns that stand for things or people that are the direct object of the verb (i.e. what or who is receiving the action of the verb). In English, you find them after the verb.

Singular	
me	*me*
te	*you*
lo	*him / it, you (m formal)*
la	*her / it, you (f formal)*

Plural	
nos	*us*
os	*you*
los	*them (m) / you (m formal)*
las	*them (f) / you (f formal)*

Indirect object pronouns

These are the pronouns that stand for things or people that are the **indirect** object of the verb. This means that they will have (or could have) the word 'to' in front of them. For example: 'He sent me a message.' (He sent a message **to me**.)

Singular	
me	*(to) me*
te	*(to) you*
le	*(to) him / her / it, you (formal)*

Plural	
nos	*(to) us*
os	*(to) you*
les	*(to) them / you (formal)*

Reflexive pronouns

These are the pronouns used with reflexive verbs (see **page 65**), verbs whose subject is the same as the object. E.g. 'I enjoyed **myself**.' (The subject is 'I'; the object is 'myself'.)

Singular	
me	*myself*
te	*yourself*
se	*himself / herself / itself, yourself (formal)*

❶ Plural	
nos	*ourselves*
os	*yourselves*
se	*themselves / yourselves (formal)*

In Spanish, object and reflexive pronouns go before most verbs:
Lo vi. → *I saw it.*   **Te he escrito.** → *I have written to you.*   **Me levantaré.** → *I'll get up.*

With an infinitive, they can go before the first verb or on the end of the infinitive.
Lo voy a comprar. / Voy a comprarlo. → *I am going to buy it.*

With commands (the imperative), they go on the end.
Mándame la foto. → *Send me the photo.*

❶ The plural reflexive pronouns can indicate 'each other':
Se besaron. → *They kissed each other.*   **Nos entendemos.** → *We understand each other.*

> **!** You will know when a verb is reflexive because it will appear in vocabulary lists with **se** on the end, e.g. **lavarse** *to have a wash*, **levantarse** *to get up*.

Relative pronoun: que

This is a useful word to link phrases together.

que is used to mean 'who', 'that' or 'which':

Esta es mi prima, que vive en Málaga.   *This is my cousin, who lives in Málaga.*
Tengo el mismo profesor que tenía mi hermana.   *I've got the same teacher that my sister had.*
Leí el libro que me recomendaste.   *I read the book which you recommended.*

✚ Remember

Bear in mind that, in Spanish, the word **que** is not optional like it is in English.
This is the dress (that) I bought yesterday.   **Este es el vestido que compré ayer.**

⊕ Higher Tier

Lo que

Lo que means 'what' when it refers to a general idea (when it is not a question).

Eso es lo que voy a hacer.
That is what I am going to do.
Lo que me gusta más es nadar.
What I like best is swimming.

Cuando, donde

As well as being question words, these words are useful link words to connect two ideas. When used this way, they do not have accents.

No me gustaban las verduras cuando era pequeño.
I didn't used to like vegetables when I was little.
Este es el armario donde puedes poner tu ropa.
This is the wardrobe where you can put your clothes.

el que, la que, los que, las que

These pronouns are used after prepositions (e.g. **a**, **en**, **de**, **por**, **con**) to refer to both people and things. After a preposition, they mean 'which'.

They can also be translated as 'the one(s) that'.

Note how they always reflect the number and gender of the noun they refer to.

Esta es la bicicleta en la que gané mi primera carrera.
This is the bike on which I won my first race.
Voy a llevar la camiseta azul, la que compré el sábado.
I am going to wear the blue T-shirt, the one that I bought on Saturday.

You may also see the more formal version of **el que** etc. (**el cual, la cual, los cuales, las cuales**).
Estas son las razones por las cuales voy a dejar mi trabajo.
These are the reasons due to which I am going to leave my job.

ⓗ Possessive pronouns

These words indicate possession or ownership and replace the noun to which they refer. For example: 'This coffee is yours' ('yours' = your coffee). They agree with the noun that they replace.

	masculine singular	masculine plural	feminine singular	feminine plural
mine	el mío	los míos	la mía	las mías
yours (s)	el tuyo	los tuyos	la tuya	las tuyas
his / hers / its	el suyo	los suyos	la suya	las suyas
ours	el nuestro	los nuestros	la nuestra	las nuestras
yours (pl)	el vuestro	los vuestros	la vuestra	las vuestras
theirs	el suyo	los suyos	la suya	las suyas

Aquí vienen las maletas, y esa es la mía. *Here come the suitcases, and that one is mine.*

Miguel tiene su billete; yo tengo los nuestros. *Miguel has his ticket; I've got ours.*

ⓗ Prepositional pronouns

These are pronouns which must be used after a preposition (e.g. **a**, **en**, **con**, **por**, **de**).

For example: 'This is for you.' 'She went with them.'

mí	*me*
ti	*you (singular)*
él	*him / it*
ella	*her / it*
usted	*you (formal, singular)*

nosotros /-as	*us*
vosotros /-as	*you (plural)*
ellos	*them (m)*
ellas	*them (f)*
ustedes	*you (formal, plural)*

> **!** Note the irregular forms with **con** (*with*): **conmigo** *with me*, **contigo** *with you*.

Tengo un regalo para ti. *I have a present for you.*

No voy a ir sin ellos. *I am not going to go without them.*

These are also used for emphasis, in addition to the object pronoun, and are preceded by **a**.

Elena quiere ver la película, pero a mí no me interesa.
*Elena wants to see the film but **I'm** not interested.*

Te di la entrada a ti, no a él.
*I gave the ticket to **you**, not to him.*

VERBS AND TENSES

The infinitive

The infinitive is the basic form of the verb, the starting point, and in English starts with 'to ...'. For example, 'to make', 'to see', 'to be'.

In Spanish, infinitives fall into three categories:

those ending in **-ar**	**hablar** *to talk / speak*, **ganar** *to earn / win*
those ending in **-er**	**comer** *to eat*, **beber** *to drink*
those ending in **-ir**	**vivir** *to live*, **escribir** *to write*

The present tense

This tense is used for actions that are taking place now or take place regularly in the present.

En este momento, hago mis deberes.   *At the moment, I am doing my homework.*
Vivo en el norte de España.   *I live in the north of Spain.*
Tomamos el desayuno en la cocina.   *We have breakfast in the kitchen.*

The endings change depending on who is doing the action. The endings also differ depending on which category of verb is used: **-ar**, **-er** or **-ir**.

Most verbs follow this regular pattern:
Remove the infinitive ending (**-ar**, **-er** or **-ir**) and add the following endings:

	-ar hablar *to talk*		**-er** comer *to eat*		**-ir** vivir *to live*	
yo	-o	habl**o**	-o	com**o**	-o	viv**o**
tú	-as	habl**as**	-es	com**es**	-es	viv**es**
él / ella / usted	-a	habl**a**	-e	com**e**	-e	viv**e**
nosotros / -as	-amos	habl**amos**	-emos	com**emos**	-imos	viv**imos**
vosotros / -as	-áis	habl**áis**	-éis	com**éis**	-ís	viv**ís**
ellos / ellas / ustedes	-an	habl**an**	-en	com**en**	-en	viv**en**

> **!** Note the irregular first person singular (**yo**) forms of these verbs:
>
>   **dar → doy** *I give*   **saber → sé** *I know*   **poner → pongo** *I put*   **conocer → conozco** *I know*
>
> **🅗 Higher only:** Verbs ending in **-ger** change to **-jo** in the first person singular:
>
>   **coger → cojo** *I catch*

Common irregular verbs in the present tense

	ser *to be*	estar *to be*	ir *to go*	tener *to have*	hacer *to do / make*
yo	soy	estoy	voy	tengo	hago
tú	eres	estás	vas	tienes	haces
él / ella / usted	es	está	va	tiene	hace
nosotros / -as	somos	estamos	vamos	tenemos	hacemos
vosotros / -as	sois	estáis	vais	tenéis	hacéis
ellos / ellas / ustedes	son	están	van	tienen	hacen

Radical-changing verbs

There are a number of verbs that change their spelling in the stem of some parts of the verb in the present tense. (The stem is the part of the verb before the infinitive ending.)

There are three categories of radical-changing verbs: those where the **e** changes to **ie**, those where the **o** changes to **ue** and those where the **e** changes to **i**.

	pensar *to think* e → ie	poder *to be able* o → ue	pedir *to ask for* e → i
yo	pienso	puedo	pido
tú	piensas	puedes	pides
él / ella / usted	piensa	puede	pide
nosotros / -as	pensamos	podemos	pedimos
vosotros / -as	pensáis	podéis	pedís
ellos / ellas / ustedes	piensan	pueden	piden

! Notice how only four parts of the verb are affected, the three singular parts and the third person plural. Also remember that the endings are not affected – they follow the pattern of regular **-ar**, **-er** and **-ir** verbs.

The verb **jugar** is unusual in that it is the **u**, instead of an **o**, that changes to **ue**.

+ Remember

When you come across a radical-changing verb, write it down in your vocabulary book like this: **preferir (ie)**. Then you will know which letter changes and what it changes to.

The present continuous tense

This tense is the equivalent of the English 'to be -ing' ('I am waiting', 'she is writing'). It indicates that the action of the verb is happening at the time of speaking.

It is formed by the present tense of **estar** (**estoy, estás, está, estamos, estáis, están**) and the present participle (also known as the gerund).

Forming the present participle (gerund)

ar verbs	remove the infinitive ending and add **-ando** **hablar → hablando** *speaking / talking*
er / ir verbs	remove the infinitive ending and add **-iendo** **comer → comiendo** *eating* **salir → saliendo** *leaving*

Están esperando en la estación.   *They are waiting at the station.*
¿Qué estás haciendo?   *What are you doing?*

Irregular present participles

Verbs whose stem ends in a vowel add a **y**.

eg	**leer** *to read* → **leyendo, caer** *to fall* → **cayendo, construir** *to build* → **construyendo**

Verbs in the **pedir** family change **e** to **i**.

eg	**pedir** *to ask for* → **pidiendo, mentir** *to lie* → **mintiendo, repetir** *to repeat* → **repitiendo**

The preterite tense

This tense is used to talk about a single, completed event in the past.
For example: 'Yesterday **I made** dinner for the family.'

Regular verbs: remove the infinitive ending and add the following endings:

	-ar hablar *to talk*	-er comer *to eat*	-ir vivir *to live*
yo	habl**é**	com**í**	viv**í**
tú	habl**aste**	com**iste**	viv**iste**
él / ella / usted	habl**ó**	com**ió**	viv**ió**
nosotros / -as	habl**amos**	com**imos**	viv**imos**
vosotros / -as	habl**asteis**	com**isteis**	viv**isteis**
ellos / ellas / ustedes	habl**aron**	com**ieron**	viv**ieron**

 Note that **-er** verbs and **-ir** verbs have the same endings.

Verbs in the preterite with irregular stems

The following verbs (shown here in the first person singular of the preterite) have an irregular stem and then follow a particular pattern of endings.

estar → estuve	tener → tuve	poder → pude	hacer → hice	venir → vine
poner → puse	querer → quise	decir → dije	traer → traje	

Endings

tuve	tuvimos
tuviste	tuvisteis
tuvo	tuvieron

Note that the third personal singular of **hacer** is **hizo** (z instead of **c**) and the third person plural of **decir** and **traer** lose the **i**: **dijeron, trajeron**.

The verbs **ir**, **ser** and **dar** are irregular and are listed in the verb tables starting on **page 164**.

Ⓗ Verbs with stem changes in the first person singular preterite

Some verbs change their spelling in the first person singular of the preterite in order to preserve their pronunciation.

-zar verbs change the **z** to a **c**: **empecé** (empezar) *I started*
also **comenzar** *to start / begin*, **organizar** *to organise*, **utilizar** *to use*

-car verbs change the **c** to **qu**: **practiqué** (practicar) *I practised*
also **buscar** *to look for*, **sacar** *to take out*, **explicar** *to explain*

-gar verbs add a **u**: **llegué** (llegar) *I arrived*
also **jugar** *to play*, **pagar** *to pay*, **navegar** *to surf / browse*

⊕ Verbs with third person singular and plural changes in the preterite

Some verbs have a spelling change in the stem before the usual endings are added.

pedir *to ask for* e → i	**dormir** *to sleep* o → u	**leer** *to read* add **y**
pedí	dormí	leí
pediste	dormiste	leíste
pidió	durmió	leyó
pedimos	dormimos	leímos
pedisteis	dormisteis	leísteis
pidieron	durmieron	leyeron

Note that only the third person singular and plural are affected. Other verbs that follow this pattern are:

e → i: mentir, servir, repetir, divertir, vestir, sentir

o → u: morir

add y: caer, construir, creer, oír

The perfect tense

The perfect tense is used to say what you have done ('has / have -ed'). For example, 'I have worked', 'they have listened'. In English, we form it from the verb 'to have' and the past participle. The past participle usually ends in '-ed' in English, but there are lots of irregulars, like 'written', 'spoken', 'flown', 'caught', etc.).

The verb **haber** (not **tener**) is used for *'to have'* when forming tenses.

You need the present tense of **haber**:

haber	
he	*I have*
has	*you (s) have*
ha	*he / she / it has; you (formal) have*
hemos	*we have*
habéis	*you (pl) have*
han	*they / you (formal) have*

+

Followed by the past participle:

-ar verbs:
remove **-ar** and add **-ado**

-er / -ir verbs:
remove **-er / -ir** and add **-ido**

eg
trabajar → trabajado *worked*
comer → comido *eaten*
vivir → vivido *lived*

Put the two together:

he comprado *I have bought*   **¿Has comido?** *Have you eaten?*   **Han ido.** *They have gone.*

⊕ Irregular past participles

cubrir *to cover* → **cubierto** *covered*	**decir** *to say / tell* → **dicho** *said / told*
escribir *to write* → **escrito** *written*	**hacer** *to do / make* → **hecho** *done / made*
poner *to put* → **puesto** *put*	**ver** *to see* → **visto** *seen*
volver *to go back / return* → **vuelto** *gone back / returned*	

+ Remember

Word order

Never split the two parts of the perfect tense. In English we can say 'I have always lived in London'. In Spanish the adverb **siempre** (*always*) must go before the two parts of the tense:

Siempre he vivido en Londres.

The imperfect tense

The imperfect tense is used to describe what someone or something was like in the past, or what used to happen in the past.

For example: **Cuando era pequeño, vivía en una casa blanca.**
When I was little, I used to live in a white house.

Regular verbs: remove the infinitive ending and add the following endings:

	-ar **hablar** *to talk*	**-er** **comer** *to eat*	**-ir** **vivir** *to live*	
yo	habl**aba**	com**ía**	viv**ía**	
tú	habl**abas**	com**ías**	viv**ías**	Note that **-er** verbs and **-ir** verbs have the same endings.
él /ella / usted	habl**aba**	com**ía**	viv**ía**	
nosotros / -as	habl**ábamos**	com**íamos**	viv**íamos**	
vosotros / -as	habl**abais**	com**íais**	viv**íais**	
ellos / ellas / ustedes	habl**aban**	com**ían**	viv**ían**	

There are only three irregular verbs in the imperfect in Spanish.

	ser *to be*	**ir** *to go*	**ver** *to see*	
yo	era	iba	veía	
tú	eras	ibas	veías	**hay** *there is / are*
él / ella / usted	era	iba	veía	↓
nosotros / -as	éramos	íbamos	veíamos	**había** *there was / were*
vosotros / -as	erais	ibais	veíais	
ellos / ellas / ustedes	eran	iban	veían	

+ Remember

You use the imperfect tense to describe what the weather was / used to be like in the past.
Hacía calor pero llovía. *It was hot but it rained.*

The imperfect continuous tense

This is used to describe what 'was' happening in the past. It often appears with a preterite tense.

Estaba corriendo cuando vi a mi amigo. *I was running when I saw my friend.*

The imperfect continuous is formed by the imperfect tense of **estar** (**estaba**, **estabas**, **estaba**, **estábamos**, **estabais**, **estaban**) + the present participle (also known as the gerund). See **page 150** to remind yourself how to form the present participle.

The immediate future tense

This tense is equivalent to the English 'going to …' and it expresses what you are going to do or what is going to happen.

The immediate future is formed by:
the present tense of **ir** (**voy**, **vas**, **va**, **vamos**, **vais**, **van**) + **a** + an infinitive.

Voy a estudiar en el extranjero. *I am going to study abroad.*

Mis padres van a salir a cenar. *My parents are going to go out for dinner.*

The future tense

The future tense expresses what 'will' happen.

Después del colegio, iré a la universidad. *After school, I will go to university.*

Mi hermano hará todos sus deberes el sábado. *My brother will do all his homework on Saturday.*

This tense is formed by adding the endings to the full infinitive, without removing the **-ar** / **-er** / **-ir**. The endings are the same for all verbs.

	-ar hablar *to talk*	**-er** comer *to eat*	**-ir** vivir *to live*
yo	hablar**é**	comer**é**	vivir**é**
tú	hablar**ás**	comer**ás**	vivir**ás**
él / ella / usted	hablar**á**	comer**á**	vivir**á**
nosotros / -as	hablar**emos**	comer**emos**	vivir**emos**
vosotros / -as	hablar**éis**	comer**éis**	vivir**éis**
ellos / ellas / ustedes	hablar**án**	comer**án**	vivir**án**

There are a few verbs which have irregular stems in the future, but the endings are the same as those of regular verbs.

tener *to have* → **tendré** *I will have* **hacer** *to do* → **haré** *I will do*

poder *to be able* → **podré** *I will be able* **poner** *to put* → **pondré** *I will put*

The future of **hay** *there is / there are* is also irregular: **habrá** *there will be*.

Ⓗ Higher examples include:

querer *to want* → **querré** *I will want* **venir** *to come* → **vendré** *I will come*

saber *to know* → **sabré** *I will know* **decir** *to say* → **diré** *I will say*

salir *to go out* → **saldré** *I will go out*

The conditional

The conditional expresses what 'would' happen.

Me encantaría estudiar francés. *I would love to study French.*
Sería posible vivir aquí. *It would be possible to live here.*

 Remember

Sometimes in English 'would' is used to talk about what 'used to' happen (e.g. 'When I was little, I would play football in the park'). In Spanish you need the imperfect tense for this (**Cuando era pequeño, jugaba al fútbol en el parque**).

The conditional is formed by adding the endings to the full infinitive, without removing the **-ar** / **-er** / **-ir**. The endings are the same for all verbs, and they are the same as the endings for **-er** / **-ir** verbs in the imperfect.

	-ar **hablar** *to talk*	**-er** **comer** *to eat*	**-ir** **vivir** *to live*
yo	hablar**ía**	comer**ía**	vivir**ía**
tú	hablar**ías**	comer**ías**	vivir**ías**
él / ella / usted	hablar**ía**	comer**ía**	vivir**ía**
nosotros / -as	hablar**íamos**	comer**íamos**	vivir**íamos**
vosotros / -as	hablar**íais**	comer**íais**	vivir**íais**
ellos / ellas / ustedes	hablar**ían**	comer**ían**	vivir**ían**

The irregular stems are the same as for the future tense.

tener *to have* → **tendría** *I would have* **hacer** *to do* → **haría** *I would do*
poder *to be able to* → **podría** *I would be able to* **poner** *to put* → **pondría** *I would put*

The conditional of **hay** *there is / there are* is also irregular: **habría** *there would be.*

ⓗ Higher level examples include:

querer *to want* → **querría** *I would want* **venir** *to come* → **vendría** *I would come*
saber *to know* → **sabría** *I would know* **decir** *to say* → **diría** *I would say*
salir *to go out* → **saldría** *I would go out*

The imperative

The imperative is used to give instructions or commands, and it only exists in the 'you' forms of the verb.

For regular verbs, it is the same as the he/she/it form of the verb. See **page 125**.

Examples: ¡Espera! *Wait!* ¡Corre! *Run!* ¡Escribe! *Write!*

Some verbs are irregular in the imperative:

ser → sé	tener → ten	hacer → haz	poner → pon
ir → ve	venir → ven	decir → di	salir → sal

H For the **vosotros/as** form, remove the **-r** from the infinitive and replace it with a **-d**. There are no irregular verbs for **vosotros/as**:

Venid a mi casa. *Come to my house.*
Haced la compra. *Do the shopping.*

H The subjunctive

The subjunctive is a form of the verb that is used when there is an element of doubt, unfinished action, wishing, emotion, etc.

You need a subjunctive:

- After the future conjunction **cuando** when the action described by the verb has not yet happened.
  Iré a la universidad cuando termine el colegio. *I will go to university when I finish school.*

- After verbs of wishing, commanding, requesting and emotion.
  Quiero que comas conmigo. *I want you to eat with me.*
  Te pido que hagas tus deberes. *I'm asking you to do your homework.*
  Estoy triste de que no estudie. *I'm sad that he / she doesn't study.*

- To express purpose after **para que.**
  Te doy dinero para que compres un libro. *I'm giving you (some) money so that you can buy a book.*

To form the present subjunctive, take the **yo** form of the present tense and replace the **-o** with the following endings:

	hablar *to talk*	**comer** *to eat*	**vivir** *to live*	
yo	hable	coma	viva	
tú	hables	comas	vivas	You are only required to know the singular forms.
él / ella / usted	hable	coma	viva	
nosotros / -as	hablemos	comamos	vivamos	
vosotros / -as	habléis	comáis	viváis	
ellos / ellas / ustedes	hablen	coman	vivan	

··· The subjunctive continued

Some common verbs that have an irregular stem in the subjunctive are:

hacer → haga	**Quiero que hagas tu cama.** *I want you to make your bed.*
ser → sea	**Cuando sea mayor, seré abogado.** *When I'm older, I'll be a lawyer.*
ir → vaya	**No quiero que vayas a la playa.** *I don't want you to go to the beach.*
venir → venga	**Espero que mi padre venga hoy.** *I hope my father comes today.*
tener → tenga	**Cuando tenga veinte años, viviré en España.** *When I'm 20, I'll live in Spain.*

Reflexive verbs

These verbs need a pronoun in front of the conjugated verb. They can be recognised because they have **se** at the end of the infinitive. They often describe actions that you do to yourself, e.g. **levantarse** *to get (yourself) up*, **lavarse** *to have a wash*, **vestirse** *to get dressed*.

Reflexive verbs are not necessarily irregular verbs (some are and some are not). They have the same endings as any other verb, but with the pronoun in front.

	lavarse *to have a wash*
yo	**me** lavo
tú	**te** lavas
él / ella / usted	**se** lava
nosotros / -as	**nos** lavamos
vosotros / -as	**os** laváis
ellos / ellas / ustedes	**se** lavan

Modal verbs

Modal verbs express concepts like ability, permission, necessity, possibility and obligation. In Spanish these verbs are always followed by the infinitive.

deber *must / to have to*	querer *to want*	saber *to know*	poder *to be able to*	tener que *to have to*

Other verb forms with a similar meaning are:

quisiera *I would like*	me gustaría *I would like*	hay que *one has to*

Debo aprender el vocabulario. *I must / have to learn the vocabulary.*

Mi madre quiere vivir en Francia. *My mother wants to live in France.*

Quisiera comprar una casa enorme. *I would like to buy a huge house.*

The passive

H The passive is used when the emphasis is on the action being done, not necessarily the person doing it. It is much more common in English than in Spanish.

It is formed from **ser** (in the appropriate tense) followed by the past participle (see **page 152** to remind yourself how to form the past participle and to revise irregular ones). The past participle in the passive voice must agree with the subject.

La casa fue comprad**a** (por el hombre). *The house was bought (by the man).*

Los platos fueron cocinad**os**. *The dishes were cooked.*

H Another way of conveying the same idea is to put the pronoun **se** in front of the third person singular or third person plural verb. You cannot use this form if the verb is followed by 'by …'.

Se venden verduras aquí. *Vegetables are sold here.*

Se habla español en esta clase. *Spanish is spoken in this classroom.*

Impersonal verbs

The most common verbs of this type in Spanish are **gustar** *to like* (literally, *to please*) and **encantar** *to love*. When they are conjugated, the verb does not agree with the subject, but with the object that follows it, and they need an indirect object pronoun in front.

Me gustan los perros. *I like dogs.* (Literally, *They please me, dogs.*)

Optional pronoun	gustar *to like*
(a mí)	me gusta(n)
(a ti)	te gusta(n)
(a él / ella)	le gusta(n)
(a nosotros/as)	nos gusta(n)
(a vosotros/as)	os gusta(n)
(a ellos / ellas)	les gusta(n)

They can also have **a** + an optional extra pronoun before the indirect object pronoun, for emphasis.

A mí, me encanta el alpinismo. *I love rock climbing.*

⋯ Impersonal verbs continued

Some common verbs belonging in this category are **preocupar** *to worry*, **molestar** *to annoy*, **interesar** *to be interested in*.

¿Te interesan las matemáticas? *Are you interested in maths?*

Me preocupa el acoso. *Bullying worries me.*

ⓗ Other verbs that work in the same way are:

parecer *to seem*	**faltar** *to lack / miss*	**valer / merecer la pena** *to be worth*
bastar *to be enough*	**hacer falta** *to need*	

Ser and estar

Both of these verbs mean 'to be'.

'to be' + noun – always use **ser**:

Mi padre es profesor. *My father is a teacher.*

Soy una mujer. *I am a woman.*

'to be' + adjective:

Ser describes what someone or something is, something that is unlikely to change overnight.

España es bonita. *Spain is beautiful.*

Mi casa es azul. *My house is blue.*

Estar describes the location of someone or something, or it describes a condition that may change.

Madrid está en el centro de España. *Madrid is in the centre of Spain.*

Mis padres están nerviosos. *My parents are (feeling) nervous.*

 Some adjectives change meaning depending on whether they are used with **ser** or **estar**, see **page 139**.

Expressions with tener

Tener normally means 'to have', but it is also used in a wide range of expressions where English would use 'to be'.

tener frío / calor *to be cold / hot*	**tener miedo** *to be scared*	**tener hambre / sed** *to be hungry / thirsty*	**tener suerte** *to be lucky*

PREPOSITIONS

Prepositions go before a noun, pronoun or infinitive and express a relationship to another element in the sentence.

Fui de vacaciones con mis amigos. *I went on holiday with my friends.*

Aprobé sin estudiar demasiado. *I passed without studying too much.*

Common prepositions

The most important prepositions in Spanish are:

a *to / at*	**debajo** *underneath / below*	**entre** *between*	**por** *for / around / because of / by*
con *with*	**desde** *from / since*	**hacia** *towards*	**según** *according to*
contra *against*	**durante** *during*	**hasta** *up to / until*	**sin** *without*
de *of / from*	**en** *in / on*	**para** *for / in order to*	**sobre** *on top / over / about*

Ⓗ Antes de / después de

To indicate sequence, these can be used followed by an infinitive.

Antes de salir, voy a llamar a mi abuela. *Before going out, I'm going to call my grandmother.*

Después de desayunar, fui al colegio. *After having breakfast, I went to school.*

Por vs para

Both of these can mean 'for'. **Por** expresses a reason why, or translates as 'through', whereas **para** shows purpose or intention.

Por

por tu salud *because of your health*
por el parque *through the park*

Para

un regalo para ti *a present for you*
para tener buenas notas *in order to have good grades*

Personal a

When the object of the verb is a person, you need to include the preposition **a** before it.

Vi a tu madre en el centro. *I saw your mother in the centre.*

Voy a llamar a mi amigo. *I am going to call my friend.*

Verbs followed by prepositions

Many Spanish verbs must be followed by a particular preposition. The preposition does not always correspond to the English equivalent, so you will need to learn them.

Verbs followed by **a**	
aprender a	*to learn to*
atreverse a	*to dare to*
ayudar a	*to help to*
empezar a	*to start to*

Verbs followed by **de**	
acordarse de	*to remember to*
olvidarse de	*to forget to*
terminar de	*to finish*
tratar de	*to try to*

Verbs followed by **en**	
consistir en	*to consist of*
insistir en	*to insist on*
pensar en	*to think about*

Verbs followed by **con**	
contar con	*to count on*
soñar con	*to dream of*

There are some verbs in Spanish that change their meaning when followed by a preposition:

volver *to return*	→	**volver a** *to (do something)* *again*
dejar *to leave / allow*	→	**dejar de** *to stop* (doing something)
acabar *to finish*	→	**acabar de** *to have just* (done something)
llegar *to arrive*	→	**llegar a** *to manage to*
ir *to go*	→	**ir de** *to go for / on, to go + -ing* e.g. **ir de vacaciones** *to go on holiday*, **ir de compras** *to go shopping*

QUESTIONS

Questions can be expressed in Spanish through intonation, which turns a statement into an interrogative. You just need to add an inverted question mark at the beginning of the statement, and a question mark at the end.

Pedro nada todos los días. *Pedro swims every day.*

¿Pedro nada todos los días? *Does Pedro swim every day?*

Question words

Another way to ask a question in Spanish is to use a question word. Normally the sentence order will be inverted, by placing the verb before the subject.

¿Dónde vive Alicia? *Where does Alicia live?*

¿Cuándo vendrás a Inglaterra? *When will you come to England?*

It is really important to learn question words, especially for the speaking exam.

¿dónde?	*where?*	**¿cómo?**	*how / what ... like?*
¿(a)dónde?	*where to?*	**¿qué?**	*what / which?*
¿cuándo?	*when?*	**¿por qué?**	*why?*
¿cuál(es)?	*which / what?*	**¿quién(es)?**	*who?*
¿cuánto/a?	*how much?*	**¿de quién / quiénes?**	*whose?*
¿cuántos/as?	*how many?*	**¿a quién / quiénes?**	*to whom? / who to?*

If a question includes a preposition, the preposition needs to go before the question word:

¿Con quién estás hablando? *Who are you talking to?*

Hace / desde / desde hace

To say how long you have been doing something that you are still doing, use the verb in the present tense followed by desde hace + a period of time.

You can also use **hace** + a period of time + **que**.

Hace on its own means 'ago', but the word order is different from English.

Desde means 'since'.

Estudio español desde hace cinco años. *I have been studying Spanish for five years.*

Hace cinco años que estudio español. *I have been studying Spanish for five years.*

Empecé a estudiar español hace cinco años. *I started to study Spanish five years ago.*

Estudio español desde abril. *I have been studying Spanish since April.*

NEGATION

Negative words

To make a sentence negative, all you need to do is put **no** in front of the verb:

No me gusta el pescado. *I don't like fish.*

Other negative words allow you to add more complexity to your speaking and writing:

nada *nothing*	**nunca** *never*	**nadie** *nobody*	**ninguno** *none / no / neither / not ... any*

When using these negative words in a sentence, you still need **no** in front of the verb, except when the sentence begins with the negative word.

No hago ejercicio nunca. / Nunca hago ejercicio. *I never do exercise.*

No llegó nadie ayer. / Nadie llegó ayer. *Nobody arrived yesterday.*

No tengo ningún amigo. *I haven't got any friends.*

Try using the following if you are aiming higher:

ya no *no longer*	**tampoco** *neither*	**ni ... ni ...** *neither ... nor*

VERB TABLES

Regular -ar verbs — hablar *to speak*

	Present	Preterite	Imperfect	Future
yo	hablo	hablé	hablaba	hablaré
tú	hablas	hablaste	hablabas	hablarás
él / ella / usted	habla	habló	hablaba	hablará
nosotros / -as	hablamos	hablamos	hablábamos	hablaremos
vosotros / -as	habláis	hablasteis	hablabais	hablaréis
ellos / ellas / ustedes	hablan	hablaron	hablaban	hablarán

present participle: **hablando** *speaking*   past participle: **hablado** *spoken*

Regular -er verbs — comer *to eat*

	Present	Preterite	Imperfect	Future
yo	como	comí	comía	comeré
tú	comes	comiste	comías	comerás
él / ella / usted	come	comió	comía	comerá
nosotros / -as	comemos	comimos	comíamos	comeremos
vosotros / -as	coméis	comisteis	comíais	comeréis
ellos / ellas / ustedes	comen	comieron	comían	comerán

present participle: **comiendo** *eating*   past participle: **comido** *eaten*

Regular -ir verbs — vivir *to live*

	Present	Preterite	Imperfect	Future
yo	vivo	viví	vivía	viviré
tú	vives	viviste	vivías	vivirás
él / ella / usted	vive	vivió	vivía	vivirá
nosotros / -as	vivimos	vivimos	vivíamos	viviremos
vosotros / -as	vivís	vivisteis	vivíais	viviréis
ellos / ellas / ustedes	viven	vivieron	vivían	vivirán

present participle: **viviendo** *living*   past participle: **vivido** *lived*

Irregular verbs

Dar *to give*	Present	Preterite	Imperfect	Future
yo	doy	di	daba	daré
tú	das	diste	dabas	darás
él / ella / usted	da	dio	daba	dará
nosotros / -as	damos	dimos	dábamos	daremos
vosotros / -as	dais	disteis	dabais	daréis
ellos / ellas / ustedes	dan	dieron	daban	darán

present participle: **dando** *giving*   past participle: **dado** *given*

Decir *to say*	Present	Preterite	Imperfect	Future
yo	digo	dije	decía	diré
tú	dices	dijiste	decías	dirás
él / ella / usted	dice	dijo	decía	dirá
nosotros / -as	decimos	dijimos	decíamos	diremos
vosotros / -as	decís	dijisteis	decíais	diréis
ellos / ellas / ustedes	dicen	dijeron	decían	dirán

present participle: **diciendo** *saying*   past participle: **dicho** *said*

Empezar *to begin*	Present	Preterite	Imperfect	Future
yo	empiezo	empecé	empezaba	empezaré
tú	empiezas	empezaste	empezabas	empezarás
él / ella / usted	empieza	empezó	empezaba	empezará
nosotros / -as	empezamos	empezamos	empezábamos	empezaremos
vosotros / -as	empezáis	empezasteis	empezabais	empezaréis
ellos / ellas / ustedes	empiezan	empezaron	empezaban	empezarán

present participle: **empezando** *beginning*   past participle: **empezado** *begun*

Estar *to be*	Present	Preterite	Imperfect	Future
yo	estoy	estuve	estaba	estaré
tú	estás	estuviste	estabas	estarás
él / ella / usted	está	estuvo	estaba	estará
nosotros / -as	estamos	estuvimos	estábamos	estaremos
vosotros / -as	estáis	estuvisteis	estabais	estaréis
ellos / ellas / ustedes	están	estuvieron	estaban	estarán

present participle: **estando** *being*   past participle: **estado** *been*

Haber *to have*	Present	Preterite	Imperfect	Future
yo	he	hube	había	habré
tú	has	hubiste	habías	habrás
él / ella / usted	ha	hubo	había	habrá
nosotros / -as	hemos	hubimos	habíamos	habremos
vosotros / -as	habéis	hubisteis	habíais	habréis
ellos / ellas / ustedes	han	hubieron	habían	habrán

present participle: **habiendo** *having*   past participle: **habido** *had*

Hacer *to do / make*	Present	Preterite	Imperfect	Future
yo	hago	hice	hacía	haré
tú	haces	hiciste	hacías	harás
él / ella / usted	hace	hizo	hacía	hará
nosotros / -as	hacemos	hicimos	hacíamos	haremos
vosotros / -as	hacéis	hicisteis	hacíais	haréis
ellos / ellas / ustedes	hacen	hicieron	hacían	harán

present participle: **haciendo** *doing / making*   past participle: **hecho** *done / made*

Ir *to go*	Present	Preterite	Imperfect	Future
yo	voy	fui	iba	iré
tú	vas	fuiste	ibas	irás
él / ella / usted	va	fue	iba	irá
nosotros / -as	vamos	fuimos	íbamos	iremos
vosotros / -as	vais	fuisteis	ibais	iréis
ellos / ellas / ustedes	van	fueron	iban	irán

present participle: **yendo** *going*   past participle: **ido** *gone*

Jugar *to play*	Present	Preterite	Imperfect	Future
yo	juego	jugué	jugaba	jugaré
tú	juegas	jugaste	jugabas	jugarás
él / ella / usted	juega	jugó	jugaba	jugará
nosotros / -as	jugamos	jugamos	jugábamos	jugaremos
vosotros / -as	jugáis	jugasteis	jugabais	jugaréis
ellos / ellas / ustedes	juegan	jugaron	jugaban	jugarán

present participle: **jugando** *playing*   past participle: **jugado** *played*

Poder *to be able to*	Present	Preterite	Imperfect	Future
yo	puedo	pude	podía	podré
tú	puedes	pudiste	podías	podrás
él / ella / usted	puede	pudo	podía	podrá
nosotros / -as	podemos	pudimos	podíamos	podremos
vosotros / -as	podéis	pudisteis	podíais	podréis
ellos / ellas / ustedes	pueden	pudieron	podían	podrán

present participle: **pudiendo** *being able to*   past participle: **podido** *been able to*

Poner *to put*	Present	Preterite	Imperfect	Future
yo	pongo	puse	ponía	pondré
tú	pones	pusiste	ponías	pondrás
él / ella / usted	pone	puso	ponía	pondrá
nosotros / -as	ponemos	pusimos	poníamos	pondremos
vosotros / -as	ponéis	pusisteis	poníais	pondréis
ellos / ellas / ustedes	ponen	pusieron	ponían	pondrán

present participle: **poniendo** *putting*   past participle: **puesto** *put*

Querer to want	Present	Preterite	Imperfect	Future
yo	quiero	quise	quería	querré
tú	quieres	quisiste	querías	querrás
él / ella / usted	quiere	quiso	quería	querrá
nosotros / -as	queremos	quisimos	queríamos	querremos
vosotros / -as	queréis	quisisteis	queríais	querréis
ellos / ellas / ustedes	quieren	quisieron	querían	querrán

present participle: **queriendo** *wanting*   past participle: **querido** *wanted*

Saber to know	Present	Preterite	Imperfect	Future
yo	sé	supe	sabía	sabré
tú	sabes	supiste	sabías	sabrás
él / ella / usted	sabe	supo	sabía	sabrá
nosotros / -as	sabemos	supimos	sabíamos	sabremos
vosotros / -as	sabéis	supisteis	sabíais	sabréis
ellos / ellas / ustedes	saben	supieron	sabían	sabrán

present participle: **sabiendo** *knowing*   past participle: **sabido** *known*

Sacar to get / take out	Present	Preterite	Imperfect	Future
yo	saco	saqué	sacaba	sacaré
tú	sacas	sacaste	sacabas	sacarás
él / ella / usted	saca	sacó	sacaba	sacará
nosotros / -as	sacamos	sacamos	sacábamos	sacaremos
vosotros / -as	sacáis	sacasteis	sacabais	sacaréis
ellos / ellas / ustedes	sacan	sacaron	sacaban	sacarán

present participle: **sacando** *getting / taking out*   past participle: **sacado** *got / taken out*

Ser to be	Present	Preterite	Imperfect	Future
yo	soy	fui	era	seré
tú	eres	fuiste	eras	serás
él / ella / usted	es	fue	era	será
nosotros / -as	somos	fuimos	éramos	seremos
vosotros / -as	sois	fuisteis	erais	seréis
ellos / ellas / ustedes	son	fueron	eran	serán

present participle: **siendo** *being*   past participle: **sido** *been*

Tener to have	Present	Preterite	Imperfect	Future
yo	tengo	tuve	tenía	tendré
tú	tienes	tuviste	tenías	tendrás
él / ella / usted	tiene	tuvo	tenía	tendrá
nosotros / -as	tenemos	tuvimos	teníamos	tendremos
vosotros / -as	tenéis	tuvisteis	teníais	tendréis
ellos / ellas / ustedes	tienen	tuvieron	tenían	tendrán

present participle: **teniendo** *having*   past participle: **tenido** *had*

Venir to come	Present	Preterite	Imperfect	Future
yo	vengo	vine	venía	vendré
tú	vienes	viniste	venías	vendrás
él / ella / usted	viene	vino	venía	vendrá
nosotros / -as	venimos	vinimos	veníamos	vendremos
vosotros / -as	venís	vinisteis	veníais	vendréis
ellos / ellas / ustedes	vienen	vinieron	venían	vendrán

present participle: **viniendo** *coming*   past participle: **venido** *come*

Ver to see	Present	Preterite	Imperfect	Future
yo	veo	vi	veía	veré
tú	ves	viste	veías	verás
él / ella / usted	ve	vio	veía	verá
nosotros / -as	vemos	vimos	veíamos	veremos
vosotros / -as	veis	visteis	veíais	veréis
ellos / ellas / ustedes	ven	vieron	veían	verán

present participle: **viendo** *seeing*   past participle: **visto** *seen*

Volver to return	Present	Preterite	Imperfect	Future
yo	vuelvo	volví	volvía	volveré
tú	vuelves	volviste	volvías	volverás
él / ella / usted	vuelve	volvió	volvía	volverá
nosotros / -as	volvemos	volvimos	volvíamos	volveremos
vosotros / -as	volvéis	volvisteis	volvíais	volveréis
ellos / ellas / ustedes	vuelven	volvieron	volvían	volverán

present participle: **volviendo** *returning*   past participle: **vuelto** *returned*

EXAMINATION PRACTICE ANSWERS

For detail on how the exam will be marked, you can download the mark schemes from the AQA website and marking guidance from **ClearRevise.com**.

Theme 1   People and lifestyle

Reading

01 B   02 A   03 B   05 C   [4 marks]

05 M + G   06 M + G   07 M   08 G   09 M   10 G   [6 marks]

11   Translation into English.   [4 marks]

Spanish	Model answer	Accept	Reject	Mark
Tengo mucha suerte	I am very lucky	really lucky	I have luck	1
de tener un amigo como Martín.	to have a friend like Martín.		of having	1
Es muy comprensivo y	He is very understanding and		comprehensive	1
puedo confiar en él.	I can trust him.	confide in him		1

Listening

01 B   02 E   03 D   04 H   05 A   06 G   [6 marks]

	Model answer	Accept	Reject	Mark
07	was compulsory	was obligatory		1
08	some of her friends would do no exercise	some friends wouldn't do any exercise		1
09	homework three times a week	three lots of homework a week	too much homework	1
10	water sports outdoor activities	aquatic sports activities in the open air		1 1

Dictation (10 marks)

11   Voy a estudiar / cuatro asignaturas / en septiembre.
12   Nuestra corbata / tiene / rayas amarillas.
13   Esta naranja / es dulce.
14   Mi hermana / intenta comer / menos carne roja.
15   La calidad / de la enseñanza / es excelente.

Speaking

Role play

Examples of answers and marks awarded: [10 marks]

	2 marks	1 mark	0 marks
01	Mi mejor amigo/a es alto/a.	Rubio amigo.	Amigo pakeeno. (mispronunciation of **pequeño**)
02	Es muy divertido/a.	Simpático.	Muy amigo.
03	Me gusta el instituto.	Gusto el instituto.	Colledgio grand. (mispronunciation of **colegio grande**)
04	Mi asignatura favorita es la biología.	Favorito ... inglés.	España.
05	¿Cómo es tu familia?	Tu familia ¿grande?	¿Familia?

Reading aloud task (5 marks; conversation 10 marks)
06   Check your pronunciation by listening to the **recording**.   [5 + 10 marks]

TRACK 88

Photo card

07 Response to content of photos. [5 marks]

Listen to the **recording** to hear an example of a student talking about the two photos.

08 Photo card unprepared conversation. [20 marks]

Listen to the **recording** to hear an example of a student answering the questions.

TRACK 89

TRACK 90

Writing

01 **50**-word writing task (Foundation) [10 marks]

Example:

Los profesores en mi colegio son simpáticos y trabajadores.
Mi asignatura favorita es la geografía porque es interesante.
En mi colegio hay muchos laboratorios pero no hay piscina.
La comida del colegio es muy buena pero un poco cara.
En el recreo juego al fútbol con mis amigos o charlamos. **[50 words]**

02 Translation into Spanish. For mark allocation, see guidance on getting top marks. [10 marks]

English	Model answer	Accept	Reject
She has	Tiene		
fair hair and	el pelo rubio y		
she wears glasses.	lleva gafas.	tiene gafas	
Sometimes	A veces		
I fight with	me peleo con	discuto con	lucho con
my younger brother.	mi hermano menor.	mi hermano pequeño	
I will continue	Continuaré	Voy a continuar	
with my studies	con mis estudios		
next year.	el año que viene.	el año próximo	
The good thing is that	Lo bueno es que		
I do not have to	no tengo que		
study IT.	estudiar informática.		
I hate	Detesto	Odio	
our uniform –	nuestro uniforme –		
it is very ugly.	es muy feo.		

03 **90**-word writing task (Foundation and Higher) [15 marks]

Example:

Me gusta mucho el pescado y tomamos platos de pescado por lo menos dos veces por semana. También me gusta el pollo – hay muchas comidas que puedes cocinar con pollo. No podría ser vegetariano completamente pero no me importa probar algunos platos vegetarianos a veces.

La semana que viene voy a jugar al fútbol en el parque con mis amigos y también iré a la piscina el domingo.

La semana pasada mis amigos y yo fuimos a andar en el campo con mi perro. Llevamos la comida en las mochilas y caminamos unos diez kilómetros. **[95 words]**

04 **150**-word writing task (Higher tier) [25 marks]

Example:

Normalmente llego al instituto sobre las nueve menos diez y las clases empiezan a las nueve. Tenemos dos clases antes del recreo, cuando como la fruta que llevo de casa y charlo con mis amigos. Después, hay tres clases más y la hora de comer es a la una. Como en la cafetería del instituto y las comidas no están mal, pero parece que hay patatas fritas con todo. Tenemos dos clases más después de comer y terminamos a las tres y media.

El año que viene, voy a continuar con mis estudios en el instituto. Tenemos que elegir tres asignaturas. Yo voy a hacer inglés y teatro, pero no sé qué más, posiblemente historia o dibujo. El curso dura dos años y después creo que quiero ir a la universidad, pero no estoy segura de la carrera que haré. Estoy pensando en el periodismo, pero voy a considerar varias opciones. **[151 words]**

Reading

01 A   02 M   03 A   04 P   05 I   06 M   07 P   08 I   [8 marks]

Translation into English

	Spanish	Model answer	Accept	Reject	Mark
09	Estoy leyendo	I am reading			1
	en mi dormitorio.	in my bedroom.	in my room.		1
10	La semana pasada, hice natación	Last week, I went swimming	I did swimming		1
	en la piscina de mi pueblo.	in my town's pool.	in the swimming pool in / of my town	city	1
11	Cuando era pequeño,	When I was little,	young,	younger	1
	iba al cine con mis padres.	I used to go to the cinema with my parents.	went my dads		1
12	Antes de ir a la fiesta,	Before going to the festival / party	Before I go		1
	tengo que vestirme.	I have to get dressed.	get changed		1
13	Ningún famoso quiere	No famous person wants	No celebrity		1
	compartir toda su vida en las redes sociales.	to share their whole life on social media.	all their life		1

Listening

01 P   02 N   03 P + N   04 N   [4 marks]

05.1 A   05.2 A + B   05.3 B   05.4 B   05.5 A + B

06   **Dictation**   [10 marks]
  1. El baloncesto / es una actividad / saludable.
  2. Los famosos / viven con / demasiados lujos.
  3. La Tomatina / parece / una fiesta muy sucia.
  4. Quisiera / visitar el carnaval.
  5. Las telenovelas / me hacen dormir.

Speaking

Role play   [10 marks]
Examples of answers and marks awarded:

	2 marks	1 mark	0 marks
01	Me gustan porque son sociables.	Me gustan. Divertido.	Soy divertido.
02	¿Te gusta ver deportes en la tele? ¿Ves deportes en la tele?	¿Deportes en la tele bien?	¿Deportes ver?
03	El sonido es bueno y vas con tus amigos.	Es bueno. Bien.	Eres bueno.
04	Fuimos al parque y jugamos al fútbol.	Fuimos al parque. Fútbol..	Eres el parque.
05	Toco el piano porque es relajante.	Toco el piano. Relajante.	Es rilijinte.

Photo card
06   Listen to the **recording** to hear an example of a student talking about the two photos.   [5 marks]
07   Unprepared conversation.   [20 marks]

TRACK 91

Writing

01 Photo description [10 marks]

2 marks	1 mark	0 marks
Hay/Veo (a) cuatro / 4 personas. Hay/Veo (a) unos amigos.	cuatro personas unos amigos	cuatro (alone) Inappropriate verb + number of people, e.g. Tengo cuatro personas.
Están en el campo. Está/están de vacaciones.	estar el campo de vacaciones	campo (alone) Inappropriate verb + campo, e.g. Soy un campo.
Ríe/Ríen. Saca/sacan fotos. Tiene un teléfono. Lleva una chaqueta. Es un hombre. Es una mujer.	sacar fotos un teléfono	reír (alone) hombre (alone)
Hay/Veo montañas. Hay/Veo buen tiempo. Hay/Veo sol. Hace calor.	una montaña buen tiempo el sol	Inappropriate verb + noun, e.g. Soy una montaña. Quiero el sol.
La mujer sonríe. El hombre está contento.	la mujer sonreír hombre contento	sonreír (alone) contento (alone)

02 Translation into Spanish. For mark allocation, see guidance on getting top marks. [10 marks]

English	Model answer	Accept	Reject
I am cooking	Estoy cocinando	preparando	
dinner for my parents.	la cena para mis padres.	mis madres mi padre y mi madre	comida
I played piano	Toqué el piano		jugué tocaba
in a concert	en un concierto		
last night.	anoche.	ayer por la noche	la última / pasada noche
After the festival	Después de la fiesta	Después del festival	omission of 'de'
we could go	podríamos ir		podemos
to the beach.	a la playa.		
I no longer	Ya no		más largo
watch	veo	miro	
documentaries on TV.	documentales en la tele(visión).		documentaries telly
I think that	Creo/pienso que		omission of 'que'
celebrities should	las celebridades deberían	personas famosas gente famosa + verb in singular	
give a good example	dar (un) buen ejemplo	un ejemplo bueno	
to young people.	a los jóvenes.	a las personas jóvenes	omission of 'a'

03 **90**-word writing task (Foundation and Higher) [15 marks]
Example:
El año próximo, me gustaría celebrar mi cumpleaños con una fiesta enorme. Voy a cumplir dieciséis años, y me gustaría preparar comida riquísima y bailar con mis amigos. Será genial.

Aunque tengo muchos amigos, me gusta más cuando salgo con mi mejor amiga, que se llama Berta. Nos llevamos muy bien porque nos gustan las mismas cosas, y nos reímos mucho juntas.

Sigo a un famoso en YouTube y la semana pasada no me gustó nada porque estaba fumando y bebiendo alcohol en línea. Creo que es un ejemplo terrible. **[90 words]**

04 **150**-word writing task (Higher tier) [25 marks]

Example:

El fin de semana pasado fue terrible para mí. Salí con mis amigos al centro, pero en el parque mi móvil se cayó y ahora la pantalla está rota. Hoy en día, la tecnología es muy importante para los jóvenes, y odio estar sin mi móvil. Después, fuimos al cine para ver una película graciosa, pero no había ninguna entrada. Fuimos a comer a un restaurante italiano, pero la comida estaba fría y fue muy cara. ¡Qué desastre!

Hay algunas celebridades que dan buen ejemplo. Por ejemplo, me encanta Rafael Nadal porque, aunque es un jugador fantástico, no es orgulloso y siempre es simpático con todos. Además, Nadal ayuda a otras personas y da dinero a los niños necesitados. Muchas celebridades tienen un estilo de vida que no es bueno, y gastan su dinero en lujos que no necesitan. Por eso, me encanta Rafael Nadal, es mi persona famosa favorita. **[150 words]**

Theme 3 Communication and the world around us

Reading

01 P   02 P + N   03 N   04 P [4 marks]

	Model answer	Accept	Reject	Mark
05	You work as a team and do activities together.	The family works as a team and does things together.	Any reference to equipment.	2
06	To get in touch with nature and forget the tension(s) of urban life.	To be in contact with nature and leave behind the stress of city life.		2
07	Building a school, helping with environmental projects.	Constructing a school.		2
08	**Either:** They started a relationship while working there. **Or:** They ended up getting married.			1
09	You (will) have no energy to go on trips (or visits).			1
10	Seeking / looking for shade.	Staying in the shade.		1

Listening

01 N   02 P   03 P + N   04 P + N [4 marks]

05 2 N   06 1 F [4 marks]

07 **Dictation** [10 marks]

    1 La iglesia / está en / una plaza tranquila.
    2 Jugué / varios juegos / en línea.
    3 La pantalla / del móvil / estaba rota.
    4 No funciona / el ascensor / del hotel.
    5 El diseño / del programa / fue fatal.

Speaking

01 **Role play** [10 marks]

Examples of answers and marks awarded:

	2 marks	1 mark	0 marks
01.1	Voy a España porque hace calor.	España porque calor.	Vas España. Español.
01.2	Reservamos el hotel en línea.	Billetes de avión en ordenador.	Usaste Internet.
01.3	Vamos en avión porque es rápido.	En avión porque rápido.	En aeroplano.
01.4	Vamos a la piscina y hacemos camping en el bosque.	Vamos a la piscina.	Van parque.
01.5	¿Dónde vives? ¿Te gusta tu ciudad?	¿Tu ciudad bonito?	¿Cuándo vivir?

Reading aloud task

02 Check your pronunciation by listening to the **recording**. [5 marks]

TRACK 92 / 93

Reading aloud conversation

03 Listen to the recording to hear an example of a student answering the questions. [10 marks]

Photo card

Response to content of photos. [5 marks]

Listen to the **recording** to hear an example of a student talking about the two photos.

Photo card unprepared conversation. [20 marks]

Listen to the **recording** to hear an example of a student answering the questions.

TRACK 94 / 95

Writing

01 Translation into Spanish. For mark allocation, see guidance on getting top marks. [10 marks]

English	Model answer	Accept	Reject
I used the computer	Usé el ordenador	Utilicé / la computadora	Uso / Utilizo
to book	(para) reservar		
the flights.	los vuelos.		
María helps her grandfather	María ayuda (a) su abuelo		
to do his shopping	(a) hacer sus compras	las compras	
online.	en línea.	online.	
He was doing	Estaba haciendo	Hacía	
his homework	sus deberes		
on his laptop.	en su portátil.	el portátil el / su ordenador	
Young people	Los jóvenes	jóvenes on its own	
spend too much time	pasan demasiado tiempo		use of gastar
on their mobile phones.	en sus móviles.	en sus teléfonos.	
I forgot	Me olvidé	Olvidé	
to save	de guardar	guardar	ahorrar
my work.	mi trabajo.		

02 **90**-word writing task (Foundation and Higher.) [15 marks]

Example:

Me gusta bastante la zona donde vivo. Es tranquila con muchos árboles, pero hay tiendas también porque vivimos en las afueras de un pueblo. Mis amigos viven cerca.

Durante las últimas vacaciones, fui al sur de Inglaterra con mi familia. Nos alojamos en una casa en la costa al lado de la playa. Hizo mucho calor y nadamos en el mar todos los días.

En el futuro, me gustaría mucho ir a México. Creo que es un país muy diferente con muchas tradiciones interesantes y fiestas divertidas. También, me encanta la comida mexicana. **[93 words]**

03 **150**-word writing task (Higher tier) [25 marks]

Example:

Estoy preocupado por los problemas del medioambiente porque afectan mi zona local y también todo el planeta. Vivo en una ciudad grande y tenemos un gran problema con el tráfico. Hay demasiados coches y crean humos sucios. Por eso, respiramos aire contaminado todo el tiempo. Esto no solo es un problema en mi ciudad porque causa cambios en el clima que afecta el mundo. Cuando las temperaturas suben, esto afecta toda la vida en el planeta.

En mi instituto, aprendemos mucho sobre el medio ambiente y siempre tratamos de ahorrar energía. Apagamos las luces y las pantallas de los ordenadores. Recogemos las botellas de plástico y reciclamos papel y cartón. Cada año tenemos un Día del Medioambiente cuando vamos al insti a pie o en bici y organizamos proyectos para recoger basura. El invierno pasado, hicimos pasteles especiales para los pájaros porque no hay mucho que comer cuando hace frío. **[150 words]**

GUIDANCE ON GETTING TOP MARKS

+ Download pack

A full online version of this guidance gives you more advice on how to develop your answers progressively through the full range of marks. Download the complete pack from **ClearRevise.com**

Listening exam   Paper 1

❶ Foundation and ❶ Higher tiers | Full marks

In **Section A** of the exam, questions will either be multiple choice or they will need to be answered in English. In **Section B** you will have a dictation task where you need to write down what you hear in Spanish. For the dictation there will be about 20 words in Spanish at Foundation tier and about 30 at Higher. You will hear each item **twice** in Section A and **three** times in Section B.

Section A

In Section A, these are some of the types of question you will hear:

- **Positive/Negative/Positive + Negative.** In this type of question, you will hear what people think about something. You write P if you think it is all positive; N if it is all negative; P+N if you think there is a mixture of both. Listen very carefully. You may hear **me gusta** on the first hearing, but just check that it is not **no me gusta** when you hear it for the second time.

- **Choosing A, B or A+B.** You will hear someone speaking and you have to decide whether statement A, statement B or both A+B are correct. You may be sure that one of them is correct on the first hearing, but listen carefully on the second hearing to make sure the other statement isn't also correct.

Section B

In Section B, for the dictation, you will hear a number of short sentences in Spanish. Usually there will be **four** sentences at Foundation tier and **five** at Higher. For each sentence, this is what happens:

- you hear the whole sentence.
- you hear the sentence broken up into two or three sections.
- you hear the whole sentence again

If you hear it for the first time and there is something you miss, don't panic! You still have two more goes to get it right.

> **!** **Remember:** At the end of the exam, you have 2 minutes to check your answers in the whole paper. This gives you a chance to look again at what you have written for the dictation and to spot any careless errors you may have made.

Speaking exam　　Paper 2

The exam is divided into **three** sections which are the Role play; the Reading aloud of a text followed by 4 questions; the description of two Photo cards, followed by a conversation on the same theme as the photos. Below are some tips when you are aiming for full marks.

Role play

🅕 Foundation | Full marks

- In order to get the full 10 marks, you will need to complete the five tasks by using a verb in each case. You will usually be asked to give an opinion. **Me gusta** ('I like' or 'I like it') is often a possible verb to use. For example, if the task is 'Give your opinion of sport', you can say **Me gusta el deporte**. If you have forgotten the word **deporte**, name a sport you know the Spanish for: **Me gusta el fútbol**. This will still get two marks.

- For one of the tasks, you will have to ask a question. This can sometimes look trickier than the others. Let's say the task is 'Ask your friend a question about their school'. There are many questions you could ask, but one of them would be to ask 'Do you like your school?' (**¿Te gusta tu colegio / instituto?**).

🅗 Higher | Full marks

- Look at the advice given for Foundation tier about the task where you have to ask a question. The question-asking task at Foundation and Higher tiers is very similar as regards the level of difficulty.

- The instructions say that you must use at least one verb in each task. You may be asked to give one or two advantages or disadvantages in a task. Learn a selection of positive and negative adjectives for this kind of task. Positive ones include: **interesante** (*interesting*); **divertido** (*good fun*); **emocionante** (*exciting*); **fácil** (*easy*); **útil** (*useful*). Negative ones could be: **aburrido** (*boring*); **complicado** (*difficult, complicated*); **peligroso** (*dangerous*); **inútil** (*useless*); **caro** (*expensive*). If the task asks for two disadvantages of going to the cinema, you could say **Es aburrido y caro** (even if you think it's fantastic!).

> **!** **Remember:** In the Role play, always try to use language that you are confident you know the Spanish for. The exam is not a time to make things up unless you really have to!

Reading aloud a text

- The main difference between Foundation and Higher tiers is the length of the text. There is a minimum **35 words for Foundation** and **50 words for Higher**. There may be some words at Higher tier that are longer ones, but the pronunciation rules are always the same.
For example, the letter 'h' is always silent if it appears at the start of a word, so **hay** ('there is/there are') is pronounced like the English word 'eye', as if the 'h' at the start wasn't there.

- Practise reading Spanish aloud at home. If you get to a word that you are not sure how to pronounce, you can use a free online dictionary to help. Many of them include a function whereby clicking *Escuchar* you can listen to the word being pronounced. Some of these allow you to hear a word pronounced at half speed which can make things easier at first. You can also try typing 'pronounce ... in Spanish' on YouTube and there are several sites that will pronounce the word for you. Try it with a tricky word like **semejante** ('similar'). There will usually be more than one example. If one seems very fast, try another. AQA also have a pre-recorded sound bank of the complete vocabulary list available on the AQA website.

- If there is a longer word in the text, break it down into syllables during the preparation time before the exam and write it down on your notes sheet that you can use during the exam. For example, **entrevista** ('interview'): EN-TRAY-BEES-TA. You can then look this when **entrevista** appears in the text. Practise separating words out like this at home.

- If there is an 'e' at the end of a word, it is *always* pronounced. So, the Spanish word **horrible** could be noted down as O-REEB-LAY to show how it is pronounced.

- To get the full 5 marks for reading out the text you don't have to be perfect. Concentrate on what you see as the trickiest words and note them down as suggested above. This will help you to make as few errors as possible and you may even be perfect!

> **!** **Remember:** Take your time when reading the text. There are no extra marks for reading it quickly and, if you read it too quickly, you are more likely to mispronounce words.

Reading aloud a text — compulsory questions

After you have read the text, your teacher will ask you four questions. This is the case for **both** Foundation and Higher tiers, but the questions are slightly harder at Higher.

However, all questions at both tiers will be in the present tense and the mark scheme is the same for both tiers.

🄵 Foundation and 🄷 Higher | Full marks

- To score full marks, you must answer all questions clearly.
- Two of your answers have to contain at least three verbs. For example:
  - ¿Qué haces en tu móvil?
  - <u>Mando</u> mensajes a mis amigos, <u>escucho</u> música y <u>veo</u> vídeos (verbs underlined).
- One of your other answers must contain two verbs. For example:
  - ¿Qué piensas de los videojuegos?
  - <u>No me gustan</u> porque <u>son</u> aburridos. (verbs underlined).
- Your other answer can be as little as one word, provided it answers the question clearly. For example:
  - Describe tu móvil.
  - Negro.

Description of the photos

F Foundation | Full marks

- Try to find at least 7 or 8 things that you can identify in Spanish, then add more to get to a total of 12.

H Higher | Full marks

- Add as many other words as you can and try to get to around 15 or 16 bits of information in total.

- You can always say what is happening in the photos or what the people are doing, for example: **Hace buen tiempo y las personas están jugando al fútbol.**

Conversation

F Foundation | Full marks

- Wherever possible, give an extra piece of information when you answer a question and use a verb when you do. For example, your teacher asks you *what you do with your friends*: **¿Qué haces con tus amigos?** You could talk about some of the places where you go: **Vamos al cine y al centro comercial.** That is a good answer, but you only use one verb (**Vamos**). If you can use more than one verb, do it! For example: **Vamos al centro comercial y compramos ropa.**

- Vary what you say as much as you can and avoid repeating the same common language such as **me gusta**. You can always use **me encanta** instead or adjectives that say why you might like something: **emocionante / divertido / genial / estupendo.**

H Higher | Full marks

- Try to answer most of the questions by using at least three verbs. There will be some occasions where you feel you can go beyond three. For example, you spend a lot of time on your mobile and your teacher asks you *how you use technology*: **¿Cómo usas la tecnología?** You might think of quite a lot to say, using several verbs: **Uso mi móvil todos los días para chatear con mis amigos. Anoche llamé a mi mejor amiga y hablamos sobre los planes que tenemos para el próximo fin de semana. ¡Fue genial!** You don't have to provide very long answers too often, though.

- Your Spanish should be mostly accurate and include a wide variety of different language with some more complex structures. Learn things like **cuando sea mayor** (*when I'm older*); **acabo de ver ...** (*I've just seen ...*); **estudio español desde hace cinco años** (*I've been studying Spanish for five years*); **se debería hacer más para ...** (*we should do more in order to ...*).

In **Section A** of the exam, questions will either be multiple choice or they will need to be answered in **English**. In **Section B** you will translate some sentences from **Spanish into English**. At Foundation tier, there will be about **35** words to translate and at Higher there will be about **50**.

F Foundation and **H** Higher | Full marks

Section A

In Section A, these are some of the types of question you will see:

- **Positive / Negative / Positive + Negative.** In this type of question, you will read what people think about something. You write P if you think it is all positive; N if it is all negative; P+N if you think there is a mixture of both. Read the text carefully. You may see **es interesante**, but just check that it is not part of a negative sentence, for example **no es interesante** or **nunca es interesante**.

- **Choosing A, B or A+B.** You will read a text and you have to decide whether statement A, statement B or both A+B are correct. You may be sure that one of them is correct, but read the rest of the text carefully to make sure the other statement isn't also correct.

Section B

In Section B you have to translate some Spanish sentences into English. Don't leave any gaps. A guess always has a chance of being right; a gap doesn't. When you finish translating a sentence, read what you have written and make sure it makes sense. If it doesn't, there will be a mistake somewhere.

Question 1

Find 5 things in the photo that you definitely know the Spanish for and write 5 sentences all beginning with **Hay** (*there is/there are*), for example: **Hay una chica**. Each sentence you write is worth 2 marks.

If you can't find 5 things, you can always say what someone is doing, for example: **La mujer está trabajando**; or you may be able to say what the weather is like if the photo is outside, for example: **Hace sol**.

Question 2

You must write something that is clearly understandable about all 5 bullet points. You need to write about 50 words in total, which works out at around 10 words per bullet point. However, you can still get full marks if you write more about some of the bullet points than others.

Try to vary your language as much as you can, but it doesn't need to be complicated. For example, let's say one of the bullet points is **Comida**. You could write: **Me gusta comer pollo porque es sano. Odio las patatas fritas. Odio** (*I hate*) is used instead of **No me gusta** to avoid repeating the verb **me gusta**.

Question 3

For each question, look carefully at the three words you have to choose from. Verb endings and agreement of adjectives are always very important. For example: **Mi amiga <u>es</u> simpática** – *My (female) friend is nice*. The word for 'is', is **es** and the adjective **simpática** ends in an '*a*' because a female person is being described.

Always write the **word** you have chosen in the space and be sure to spell the word correctly, including accents, or you will not get the mark.

Question 4 (translation)

When it is marked, the translation is divided into 15 sections. Each time you translate a section accurately enough to convey the meaning, you are given a tick. The ticks are added up and you get a mark out of 5 as follows: 13–15 ticks = 5 marks; 10–12 = 4; 7–9 = 3; 4–6 = 2; 1–3 = 1. There are a further 5 marks that are given for grammatical accuracy. The exam paper doesn't show what the 15 sections are.

Have a go at everything. If you leave any blanks because you don't know a word, you will lose marks. The examiner will have to assume that if you had given it a go, you would have got it wrong anyway, so you might as well try something.

As we saw in Question 3, verb endings and adjectives are important, so always check what you have written is absolutely clear. If you make a mistake and have to correct it, cross out the incorrect word and write the other one clearly. Don't write in very small handwriting to get the correct word into a small gap because it may not be clear enough for the examiner.

Question 5

You have two questions to choose from, but you should only answer one of them. Have a good look at the bullet points in each question before you start and think which is the one where you feel most comfortable that you can write enough to use around **90** words in Spanish.

To get full marks, you will have to give clear information about all three bullet points. This means that your tense usage will have to be accurate so that you can refer to the present, past and future bullet points successfully.

You need to write around **90** words in total, which works out at about **30** words per bullet point. You won't be penalised if you write more on one bullet point than the others, but it is a good idea to have roughly the same amount of words for each one. This is because you are asked to develop your ideas regularly. For example, let's say that one bullet point asks you to write about what you do at the weekend. You could just write: **Los fines de semana voy al parque**. This is enough to cover the bullet point successfully. However, you would only be saying one thing. If you go on to write about **30** words, you will be developing your ideas, in other words writing more about what you do. Giving opinions is always a good way to develop what you write. This is what you could write: **Los fines de semana voy al parque con mis amigos. Siempre hablamos del colegio o de las redes sociales. También visito a mis abuelos, pero a veces es un poco aburrido.**

For AO3 you will need a good variety of vocabulary, so try not to repeat words wherever possible. Your writing should be as accurate as you can get it, but it doesn't have to be perfect. Vary your language, maybe by using some of these expressions:

- **sin embargo** – *however*
- **además** – *besides, also* (a good alternative to también)
- **aunque** – *although*
- **que** – *that, which* (a good way to link separate phrases to make one longer sentence - **voy a la casa de mi amigo que vive cerca del centro de la ciudad**)
- **por ejemplo** – *for example*

You will have to use three verb time frames (past, present and future) successfully so that you can write clearly about all three bullet points.

❶ Higher | Full marks

Question 1 (translation)
See the notes for Foundation Question 4. The requirements are the same at both tiers.

Question 2
See the notes for Foundation Question 5. The questions and mark scheme are identical at both tiers.

Question 3

There are **25** marks in total: **15** for AO2, which is for writing around 150 words in clearly understandable Spanish and for developing ideas and descriptions; **5** marks for AO3 range and use of language, which is for having a variety of vocabulary and grammatical structures and for being able to produce more complex language; **5** marks for AO3 accuracy, in other words the fewer mistakes you make, the better.

On AQA's website there is a copy of the mark scheme for the Higher, as well as the Foundation, papers. You will find examples of what is meant by development, variety of language and of complex language. It is a good idea to look at this so you can see what examiners will be looking for.

You have two questions to choose from, but you should only answer one of them. Have a good look at the bullet points in each question before you start. Think about which one you feel most comfortable writing enough about to use around 150 words in Spanish.

You need to write clear information in relation to both bullet points and include around 150 words. You need to develop your ideas and descriptions regularly. Giving opinions and reasons is often a good way to do this.

There must be a very good variety of vocabulary, so try to impress by including as many different words as you can.

You must use complex language regularly. Remember you can see examples on AQA's website.

The two bullet points will refer to different time frames. Usually, one point will need you to answer in the present tense and the other will refer either to the past or to the future. Make sure you have used the correct tenses and endings for the verbs in each bullet point.

INDEX

Verb types

-ar verbs 164
-er verbs 164
-ir verbs 164

A

activities 52, 54, 58
adjectives 10, 13, 53, 138
  indefinite 85, 140
adverbs 143
antes de / después de 160
appearance 10
articles 137

C

celebrations 70, 74
celebrity 76, 78, 82
Christmas 72
cinema 56
colours 4
commands 125, 156
comparatives 142
comparing 95
conditional tense 67, 155
connectors 77
customs 74

D

days of the week 2
demonstrative adjectives 140
dictation 45, 48, 73, 81, 90, 103,
  116, 132
diet 22

E

education 44
environment 124, 126, 128
exercise 24
expressions 4, 43, 159

F

fame 84
family 8, 18, 60
feminine nouns 136
festivals 66, 68, 74
films 56
first person 151
friends 16, 18
future tense 28, 39, 58, 97, 108,
  154

G

grammar 135

H

hace / desde / desde hace 162
healthy lifestyle 26
holidays 96, 98
house 118

I

immediate future tense 28, 154
imperative 125, 156
imperfect continuous tense 113,
  154
imperfect tense 58, 153
impersonal verbs 158
indefinite adjectives 85, 140
inference questions 104
infinitive 106, 148
infinitive as a noun 136
intensifiers 143
Internet 108
interview 43
introductions 8
irregular verbs 165

J

jobs 41

L

lifestyle 30

M

masculine nouns 136
mealtimes 20
Mexican festivals 68
mobile phone 106
modal verbs 80, 158
months 3

N

nationality 9, 139
negation 163
negative expressions 27
nouns 136
numbers 3

O

object pronouns 103
opinions 4, 123

P

passive 158
past continuous tense 113
past tense 108, 113
perfect tense 107, 152
personality 12
phonics 5
photo card 31, 45, 49, 55, 62,
  68, 74, 87, 91, 101, 115, 129,
  133
physical appearance 10
places 102, 104
plurals of nouns 137
por vs para 160
possessive adjectives 15, 141
possessive pronouns 147
preferences 98
prepositional pronouns 147
prepositions 69, 111, 160, 161
present continuous tense 52,
  150
present tense 16, 23, 52, 58, 82,
  108, 148
preterite tense 54, 55, 82, 150
pronouns 103, 144

EXAMINATION TIPS

When you practise examination questions, use the following tips collated from years of experience and examiner reports to help you maximise your result.

Written exams (Listening, Reading, Writing)

1. Ensure your handwriting is clear and legible.

2. Cross out any mistakes with one clear line.

3. Read the question instructions carefully.

4. **For Listening:**
   - Don't write answers while the recording is playing. Wait for the pause between the two recordings of a question or the pause between one question and the next.
   - In the dictation, you hear everything three times in total. Check your spellings when you hear each section.

5. **For Reading:**
   - Read forwards and backwards in a text from the key word in the question. Sometimes the answer comes after the key word and sometimes it comes before. Translate every word in the paragraph.

6. **For Listening and Reading:**
   - Look at the heading of the question. It is in English and gives you the question context, for example 'School'.
   - If you are asked to give a certain number of details, only give that number.
   - When answering with a letter, make sure the letter is written clearly. For example, the letter A can look like an H if you leave a gap at the top.
   - Don't leave any answers blank. A blank response will always score 0 but a guess may get a mark.

7. **For Writing:**
   - If a question asks you to write an approximate number of words, try to keep to roughly that number. If you write much more than that, you may make more errors and this can lead to a lower mark.
   - Mention all of the bullet points in an answer and tick them off on the question paper as you cover them.
   - Check that you don't miss out any parts of the translation.
   - Check your work carefully, especially verb tenses and endings.

Speaking exam

8. Use the 15 minutes preparation time wisely. You can write down exactly what you are going to say for the role play and for the description of the photos. For the reading aloud passage, you can write down tricky words as you will say them, for example *quince* as *keen-thay*.

9. You can ask for repetition of a question in any part of the test, but make sure it is in Spanish. You can say *'Repite, por favor'* or *'¿Cómo?'*.

10. Speak clearly at all times and don't read your notes from the preparation time too fast. There are no extra marks for speaking quickly.

¡Buena suerte!

New titles **coming soon!**

These guides are everything you need to ace your exams and beam with pride. Each topic is laid out in a beautifully illustrated format that is clear, approachable and as concise and simple as possible.

They have been expertly compiled and edited by subject specialists, highly experienced examiners, industry professionals and a good dollop of scientific research into what makes revision most effective. Past examination questions are essential to good preparation, improving understanding and confidence.

- Hundreds of marks worth of examination style questions
- Answers provided for all questions within the books
- Illustrated topics to improve memory and recall
- Specification references for every topic
- Examination tips and techniques
- Free Python solutions pack (CS Only)

Absolute clarity is the aim.

Explore the series and add to your collection at **www.clearrevise.com**

Available from all good book shops

amazon   X @pgonlinepub

ClearRevise
Illustrated revision and practice
AQA GCSE
Food Preparation & Nutrition
8585

ClearRevise
Illustrated revision and practice
OCR
Creative iMedia
Levels 1/2
J834 (R093, R094)

ClearRevise
Illustrated revision and practice
AQA GCSE
English Language
8700

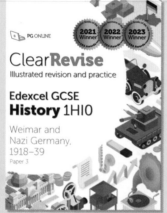

ClearRevise
Illustrated revision and practice
Edexcel GCSE
History 1HI0
Weimar and Nazi Germany, 1918–39
Paper 3

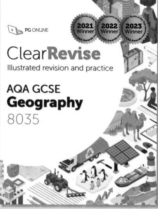

ClearRevise
Illustrated revision and practice
AQA GCSE
Geography
8035

ClearRevise
Illustrated revision and practice
OCR GCSE
Computer Science
J277

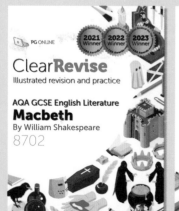

ClearRevise
Illustrated revision and practice
AQA GCSE English Literature
Macbeth
By William Shakespeare
8702

ClearRevise
Illustrated revision and practice
Edexcel GCSE
Business
1BS0

ClearRevise
Illustrated revision and practice
AQA GCSE
Combined Science
Trilogy 8464
Foundation & Higher

ClearRevise
Illustrated revision and practice
AQA GCSE
Design and Technology
8552